Early
North African
Christianity

Early North African Christianity

Turning Points in the *Development* of the *Church*

DAVID L. EASTMAN

B

Baker Academic

a division of Baker Publishing Group
Grand Rapids, Michigan

Published by Baker Academic
a division of Baker Publishing Group
PO Box 6287, Grand Rapids, MI 49516-6287
www.bakeracademic.com

Printed in the United States of America

Library of Congress Cataloging-in-Publication
Names: Eastman, David L., author.
Title: Early North African Christianity : turning points in the development of the church / David L. Eastman.
Description: Grand Rapids, Michigan : Baker Academic, a division of Baker Publishing Group, [2021] | Includes bibliographical references and index.
Identifiers: LCCN 2020058683 | ISBN 9781540963673 (paperback) | ISBN 9781540964250 (casebound)
Subjects: LCSH: Africa, North—Church history. | Church history—Primitive and early church, ca. 30–600.
Classification: LCC BR190 .E26 2021 | DDC 276/.01—dc23
LC record available at https://lccn.loc.gov/2020058683

Unless otherwise attributed, translations of ancient texts are from the author.

21   22   23   24   25   26   27   7   6   5   4   3   2   1

This book is dedicated with deep respect and gratitude to
J. Patout Burns Jr.,

renowned scholar of early African Christianity,
dear friend and colleague to many of us who are
endeavoring to pick up the mantle.
His conversations in heaven with Augustine
will be worth overhearing.

Contents

Figures

Acknowledgments

This book is based on a course that I taught in Cairo in the summers of 2014 and 2015: "Readings in Early African Christianity: Carthage and Its Vicinity." The course was taught for the Center for Early African Christianity (CEAC) under the direction of Dr. Michael Glerup and hosted by the Rev. Dr. Jos Strengholt. The students in this course provided invaluable feedback, and the CEAC has continued to provide generous support throughout the production of this volume. I would also like to express my gratitude to the late Thomas C. Oden, who was the founding director of the CEAC and who did so much to raise awareness of the early Christian history of Africa, particularly for readers outside the academy.

Kiersten Payne was my research assistant at Ohio Wesleyan University in the initial stages of moving this project from lecture to text. Her comments also contributed greatly to preparing the material for a broader reading audience.

I have also benefited from interactions with colleagues at the University of Regensburg in Germany as part of the German Research Foundation (DFG) Collaborative Research Group "Beyond Canon: Heterotopias of Religious Authority in Ancient Christianity." This international group studies the reception of canonical traditions in early Christianity. My interactions with them have informed this book's discussions of the interpretation and reception of the life and letters of the apostle Paul.

Finally, I wish to thank my dear friends and colleagues David Wilhite, Chris de Wet, Young Kim, and James Papandrea for fruitful discussions of big ideas in liminal spaces.

Abbreviations

1 Apol.	Justin, *First Apology*
Acta Cypr.	*Acts of Cyprian*
Acta mart. Scillit.	*Acts of the Scillitan Martyrs*
Adv. Donat.	Optatus of Milevis, *Against the Donatists*
Apol.	Tertullian, *Apology*
Civ.	Augustine, *The City of God*
Coll.	John Cassian, *Conferences*
Comm. Jer.	Jerome, *Commentary on Jeremiah in Six Books*
Conf.	Augustine, *Confessions*
CPD	Augustine, *To the Donatists after the Conference*
Dies nat. Pet. Paul.	Augustine, *Sermon on the Birthday of the Holy Apostles Peter and Paul*
Enchir.	Augustine, *Enchiridion (On Faith, Hope, and Love)*
Ep.	*Epistle*
Grat. Chr.	Augustine, *On the Grace of Christ and Original Sin*
Haer.	Augustine, *On Heresies*
Hist. eccl.	Eusebius, *Ecclesiastical History*
Inst.	John Calvin, *Institutes of the Christian Religion*
Jejun.	Tertullian, *On Fasting: Against the Carnal Believers*
Laps.	Cyprian, *On the Lapsed*
Mort.	Lactantius, *On the Deaths of the Persecutors*
Nupt.	Augustine, *On Marriage and Concupiscence*
Oboed.	Augustine, *On Obedience*
Orat.	Gregory of Nazianzus, *Orations*
Pass. Dat. Saturn.	*Acts of the Abitinian Martyrs*
Pass. Perp.	*Passion of Perpetua and Felicity*
Praescr.	Tertullian, *Prescription against Heretics*
Prax.	Tertullian, *Against Praxeas*
Trin.	Augustine, *On the Trinity*
Vir. ill.	Jerome, *On Illustrious Men*
Vit. Cypr.	Pontius, *Life of Cyprian*

1

A (Re)Introduction to Africa

Defining "Africa"

This book focuses on early Christian Africa, but we need to clarify what we mean by "Africa." If we say "Africa" today, many people think of the entire continent. This can create misunderstandings because when media outlets refer to problems in "Africa," they mask the great variety among the different nations on this enormous and beautiful continent. Egypt is very different from Kenya, and both of these places are quite different from South Africa.

Because we are studying the ancient world, in this book we are going to define Africa by its ancient boundaries. In our period of study, the northern coast of the continent was under the control of the <u>Roman Empire,</u> and the Romans called this particular area "Africa." <u>Africa for the Romans did not include Egypt</u> (which they just called Egypt—Aegyptus) or anywhere south of the Sahara. So in this book Africa refers not to the whole continent but to a very particular part of the northern coast of the continent.

For the sake of clarity, many scholars of early Christianity refer to this region as "<u>North Africa.</u>" They want to be more specific about what is and is not included.

The map in Figure 1.1 shows the area of Roman Africa. It stretched from modern-day Libya all the way to the northwest coast of the continent in modern-day Morocco.

Now let us look in more detail at the map of this region. In the Roman Empire, Africa was actually divided into four smaller regions for the sake of administration. Proconsular Africa covered much of modern Tunisia and

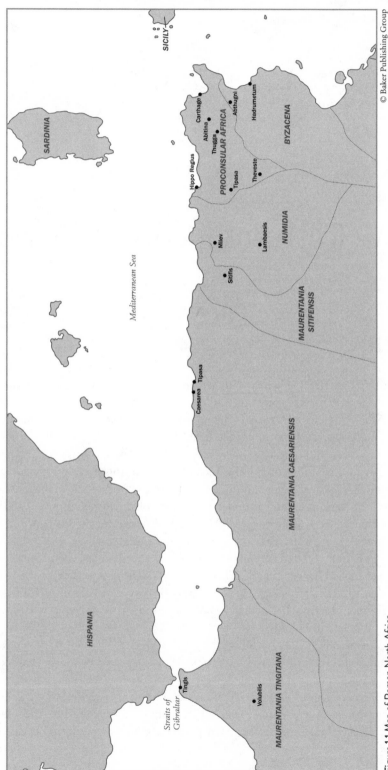

Figure 1.1 Map of Roman North Africa

northern stretches of Libya. It included Carthage, the largest and most important city in this entire region. (It was called Proconsular Africa because this was where the proconsul, or regional governor, resided.)

For a long period of time prior to Roman rule, Carthage controlled this part of the world, even including Sicily. Carthage was an ancient economic and military superpower. Because the Romans and Carthaginians kept running into each other, a series of three wars, called the Punic Wars, eventually erupted between these two empires. Rome finally came out on top, but only by a narrow margin. The famous Carthaginian general Hannibal, who marched his army across the Alps in winter (including his war elephants), very nearly conquered Rome at one point.

But Rome finally won and took over this region, and Carthage remained a key city. This was true before Christianity arrived here, and it remained true after Christianity spread throughout the Roman Empire. Carthage became one of the most significant cities in early Christianity, and the relationship between Carthage and Rome remained important and was, as we will see in this book, sometimes strained.

Farther to the west, including part of modern Algeria, was Numidia. This region also included a number of important cities. Hippo Regius ("Royal Hippo," modern Annaba) is probably the most famous. "Hippo" was a Latinized form of the city's older name in the Punic language, and "Regius" designates that the ancient kings of Numidia used to reside there.

In Christian history, Hippo's most famous resident was a bishop named Augustine (St. Augustine), who will be the focus of part 5 of this book. He served as the city's bishop from 395 or 396 CE until his death in 430. He was also born in Numidia in a place called Thagaste (modern Souk Ahras, Algeria) and studied in Madauros (modern M'Daourouch), a center of learning that was the hometown of the famous Roman author Apuleius. Overall, Numidia was less urban than Proconsular Africa, and the two regions did not always see eye-to-eye on church matters, as we will see.

Next comes the region of Mauretania, which was originally subdivided into two parts. Mauretania Caesariensis was ruled from a city called Caesarea on the Mediterranean coast, and Mauretania Tingitana was ruled from the city of Tingis (modern Tangier) on the Strait of Gibraltar. Diocletian created a third division in 293 CE, Mauretania Sitifensis (ruled from the inland city Setifis, which is modern Setif).

The regions of Mauretania were less densely populated than other parts of North Africa, but they were still home to large and impressive cities. The remains of these cities are often well preserved in the hot, dry climate of the region, but they are much less visited than other parts of the former Roman

Empire. (Travel particularly to Algeria requires a lot of planning and pa-perwork, but from personal experience I can tell you that the sites there are worth the effort. You will also have most archaeological sites and museums all to yourself.)

Africa's Centrality

When we speak of history in this period, we must be clear about another thing: Africa was at the center of the action, not an afterthought or a sec-ondary region.

By the time of the Roman Empire, the population of Rome had swelled to around one million people according to estimates by historians. According to the Jewish historian Josephus, who wrote at the end of the first century CE, about two-thirds of the wheat consumed in Rome came from Africa (the other one-third came from Egypt). Even if his math was not perfectly precise (Sicily and Sardinia also produced wheat for Rome), his point was clear: *Africa was critical to the literal survival of people living in Rome.*

As I have already mentioned, Carthage had been a full-blown superpower of the ancient world, every bit the equal of Rome in the West. Even after Rome conquered Carthage, the city did not go away. It continued to flourish for many centuries afterward, and other large cities of Africa (such as Hippo Regius, Tipasa, Curculum/Djemila, Thamugadi/Timgad, and Sitifis/Setif) also thrived, many as commercial centers.

Further proof of Africa's centrality is the name of the sea that it borders: the Mediterranean Sea.[1] "Mediterranean" in Latin means in "the middle of the earth." This sea is in the middle of everything: Rome sat on the north side of the sea that was in the middle of everything, and Carthage sat on the south side of the sea that was in the middle of everything. Even conceptually, Africa was not on the edge of the Roman world. It sat at its center.

Africa was also at the heart of the early Christian world. To convince you of this, I may first need to correct a common but incorrect idea.

In thinking about the overall historical relationship between Christianity and Africa, we need to be aware of the impact of the colonial period. There is no denying that European colonial powers did some awful things in other parts of the world, including on the continent of Africa, in their pursuit of military influence and wealth. It is also true that in some contexts the colonial powers tried to enforce their cultural values, traditions, and religion on the

---

1. During the empire, the Romans often referred to this as "Our Sea," but the name "Medi-terranean" still developed from an understanding of the importance of the area around it.

people they controlled. Any honest historian, including church historians, must acknowledge this.

However, an additional assumption is sometimes made: because European missionaries brought Christianity with them, Christianity represents colonial oppression and is not authentically African.

This assumption is categorically false. Christianity has been in Africa since the beginning. In fact, it is very likely that there were Christians in Africa before there were Christians in Europe. The man who helped Jesus carry the cross, Simon of Cyrene, was from the north coast of Africa. Very early traditions state that the apostle Matthew traveled as far south as Ethiopia, and Mark, the Gospel author, has been known as the apostle to Egypt. When it comes to Christianity, Africa did not come late to the party. Africa was there at the beginning.

The current growth of Christianity on the continent, therefore, is not something new. It is a return to the region's own roots.

Africa belongs at the center of Christian history, beginning in the early church. This is one of the main themes of this book. In the chapters that follow, I will attempt to show you the following:

1. The African church, as much as that in any other region, had to deal with the greatest threat to the survival of the early church: persecution and martyrdom.
2. African theologians and leaders undoubtedly shaped the development of Christian doctrine on core questions.
3. Some issues faced by the ancient African church are still present in parts of the Christian world today, even if in a different form.

I will not discuss every issue and every important figure in the early African church. That is beyond the scope of this project. Here we are examining only a few turning points—but turning points that are critical to understanding the development of the early church as a whole.

I divided this book into five parts: Perpetua and Felicity, Tertullian, Cyprian of Carthage, the Donatist Controversy, and Augustine of Hippo. Each part has three chapters. A part begins with a chapter introducing the historical context ("Life and Times") of the person or people involved. The two chapters that follow dive more deeply into particular issues or questions. Each chapter is introduced with a statement of the key ideas that are discussed in that chapter.

At times, the book will explore the history of some deep theological questions, but I have written in a way that will, I hope, present the main points clearly. Other theologians and historians would perhaps want me to go into the nuances of all these points, but that is not the intention of this book. Those who are interested in reading more (and more deeply) about various topics will find a list of additional resources at the back of the book.

Thank you for joining me on this journey through our past. I am excited to introduce you to some key figures who struggled, sacrificed, and even died to preserve the ancient faith that has come down to us.

Part 1

Perpetua and Felicity

2

The Life and Times of the Early Martyrs

Key Ideas

- The Romans killed Christians because they refused to worship the traditional gods and were seen as a threat to the Roman way of life.
- Other rumors spread that accused Christians of being cannibals and committing incest.
- Early periods of persecution were local and sporadic, not constant and widespread.

In this first section of the book we are going to study the *Passion of Perpetua and Felicity*, an account of the death of a group of Christians in Carthage in 202 or 203 CE. In order to set the context for this story, we need to understand the historical situation that led to the persecution of Christians. Along the way, we will also address some myths about this period of history.

I will structure the conversation in this chapter around two questions: (1) Why would Roman government officials want to kill Christians? and (2) Where and when were Christians killed? Once we understand these issues, we will be able to appreciate more fully the *Passion of Perpetua and Felicity* (and many other early Christian martyr texts).

Why Would Roman Government Officials Want to Kill Christians?

The Roman distrust and occasionally violent treatment of Christians was rooted in theology, but not in the way we might think of it. The problem was not what Christians believed, but what they did and were accused of doing or not doing.

Roman religion was fundamentally conservative and relied on a give-and-take relationship between the gods and the people. It was based on what you did, not what you believed. Coming from a Christian perspective, we might think of "religion" as a set of beliefs, but the Romans did not.

The agreement was simple: if the Romans honored the gods with the proper sacrifices, then the gods would bless them and allow Rome to survive and prosper. The relationship with the gods was described in the expression "I give so that you give" (*Do ut des*). In other words, I give an offering to a god so that the god will give me something in return. From a Roman perspective, this is how it had always been, and this had always worked. The question was not, "Do you believe in Jupiter?" Or, "How is your personal relationship with Venus?" Those questions would not have made sense to them. The question was, "Do you honor the gods with the right sacrifices done the right way?"

Failing to honor the gods was dangerous for everyone. This would anger the gods, and that could mean disaster for the Roman Empire. Whenever Rome suffered a major military defeat or natural disaster, the question was, "Which god did we offend, and how can we fix it?"

This is where Christians enter the picture. The problem was not that Christians worshiped the God of Israel and Jesus Christ as Lord. The problem was that they refused to honor the Roman gods through offering sacrifices and participating in public festivals to honor those gods. The Romans believed in many different gods, so a person could worship God or any other gods of their choosing. They just had to keep honoring the traditional Roman gods as well.

The primary charge against Christians, therefore, was atheism. Atheism? That may sound strange to our ears because modern Christians would think of ancient Romans as the ones who failed to believe in the true God. But for the Romans, the Christians were atheists because they ignored the Roman gods.

One of my favorite scenes from any martyrdom text illustrates this point. It comes from the *Martyrdom of Polycarp*, an account of the death of Polycarp, the eighty-six-year-old bishop of Smyrna (modern Izmir, Turkey). As Polycarp stood in the arena, the governor told him that he could save himself by saying, "Away with the atheists." By this the governor meant, "Away with the Christians." But Polycarp pointed to the pagan crowd and cried out,

"Away with the atheists!" He then died a horrible death, but he delivered a memorable line before he did.

For the Romans, the Christians were atheists and major threats to security. Because they refused to honor the gods, they could anger the gods. And angering the gods put the whole empire at risk. Therefore, the Christians were dangerous because of their lack of patriotism. → toward the gods

By the middle of the first century CE, the situation for Christians became more complicated, for the Roman Senate began officially declaring that some emperors who had died were now gods. There is no evidence that the members of the Senate actually believed this, but it was a ceremonial way to honor the dead emperors—at least the ones they liked. Live emperors were potential gods-to-be, so honoring the emperor with sacrifices also became a practice in Roman religion. The sacrifice was very simple. It involved taking a pinch of incense, throwing it into a fire, and saying something like, "Caesar is lord." It was not a statement of theological conviction. It was primarily a statement of patriotism to the Roman state. Failing to offer this sacrifice came to be seen as an act of treason.

All this might strike us as odd. In the United States in particular, belief in God is often tied to patriotism in a positive way. Many churches have American flags prominently displayed in their worship spaces. Support for the military is assumed in many Christian settings.

Christians "switched roles back then"

But in the first few centuries of Christianity the dynamic was quite different. Honoring Christ and not Jupiter or the emperor was considered a danger to the state. (And from the Christian side, in some periods of history members of the Roman army were not permitted to be baptized because they had sworn allegiance to the king Caesar, not the king Jesus.) Atheist Christians were seen as a threat to the public. Even harboring them could bring the wrath of the gods upon the Roman Empire.

Because of this overall suspicion and distrust of Christians, other kinds of rumors quickly spread about them. We know what some of these were thanks to a group of authors from the second century that we call the *apologists*. "Apology" (*apologia*) in Greek did not primarily mean expressing regret, as in "I apologize for being late." Offering an apology meant offering explanation or justification, so the apologists were Christian authors writing to defend and explain the beliefs and actions of Christians.

In their writings the apologists often state the charges against Christians and then explain why they were misunderstandings or simply false. Here are a few of the other popular accusations we know about:

#1   *Christians had sinister secret meetings.* The Romans as a whole were suspicious of anything done in secret. What happened in secret, after all, except things that people were trying to hide? Early church sources tell us that a public part of the Christian worship service was open to everyone, but before the celebration of the Lord's Supper, or Eucharist, those who were not baptized were required to leave. In these secret meetings people thought that the Christians were plotting to overthrow the government or doing something else dangerous.

Christians were not the only group in the empire that had private meetings. The Roman Empire had a legal category for private associations, but all associations—including religious ones—were required to be registered with the state. The Romans wanted to know who they were and what they did. Christians did not register and thus opened themselves up to even more suspicion, especially during periods of unrest or catastrophe.

#2 *Christians were cannibals.* Their own sacred texts record that their founder told his followers to eat his flesh and drink his blood. What better proof could there possibly be? Of course, this was a misunderstanding of Jesus's language at the Last Supper, but if people already believed that this group was dangerous, then it was easier to believe other bad things about them.

Even worse, this cannibalism involved eating babies. Here is a description of what some people thought happened in those "secretive" Eucharist meetings. This text comes from an author named Minucius Felix, who many historians think was from Africa. He was writing to a friend to address rumors he may have heard, such as this one:

> A young baby is covered with flour so the naïve convert is unaware of what is happening. It is then brought before the person to be admitted into their rites. The recruit is urged to strike with many blows, and this appears to be harmless because of the covering of flour. In this way the baby is killed with wounds that remain unseen and concealed. It is the blood of this infant—I shudder to mention it—that they lick with their thirsty lips. These are the limbs they distribute eagerly; this is the victim by which they seal their covenant. (*Octavius* 9)

It was thought that because Christians could not actually consume the flesh of their founder, they substituted a baby instead. The new convert killed the baby, and they all ate it.

#3 *Christians engaged in incest.* This rumor may come from the fact that Christians often greeted one another with a holy kiss—a kiss of greeting that probably resembled the greeting still common in France and other parts of the Mediterranean world. We read about this practice repeatedly in Paul's letters. And Christians used family language—calling one another brothers and sisters—to describe their relationship to one another. But from the outside perspective, Christians kissed their own brothers and sisters.

Christians did things in secret, were cannibals, and were incestuous. When added together, these rumors led to some even more disgusting accusations. Here is another passage from Minucius Felix describing an additional rumor about Christian practices:

> On a special day, they gather in a feast with all their children, sisters, mothers— all sexes and all ages. There, flushed with the banquet, after such feasting and drinking [after they have eaten the flesh and drunk the blood of the baby] they begin to burn with incestuous passions. . . . In the shameless dark with unspeakable lust they join in random unions. Everyone is equally guilty of incest, some by their actions, but everyone by allowing it to happen. (*Octavius* 9)

The Christians were accused of unspeakable acts. Even as sexually loose as the Romans were, this was still going too far for them.

You may be thinking, "How could anyone believe such crazy stories?" Try to put yourself in the place of people at that time. You are vaguely aware of this group called Christians, who are part of a new cult that comes from some distant land. They do not believe in the Roman gods, so they put everyone's safety at risk. They have secret meetings. Their texts tell them to eat flesh, drink blood, and kiss their own brothers and sisters. And there were other rumors in addition to these.

If you have heard all that, would these stories be so hard to believe? As history teaches us over and over, blind prejudice can cause people to imagine and believe many ridiculous things about people who are different from us.

And if you have heard all these stories, would you want these people living in the empire? In your city? On your street? Or would it be better for everyone if they were forced to give up their wicked ways or be eliminated altogether?

The Romans were known for many things, but failing to deal with potential threats was not one of them. Neither was mercy. If they saw a threat to their power, they used any means necessary to eliminate it. They had no hesitation about using violence. They were, after all, defending their way of life and their traditional values.

Where and When Were Christians Killed?

When I was growing up, I heard a number of things that made me think that the early Christians had been persecuted everywhere all the time. I heard about the catacombs, these secret underground places that Christians would hide to have their worship services. Only after the emperor Constantine were Christians able to come out into the light without fear of persecution.

Recently, in some popular venues, an alternative story has been told. Actually, Christians were rarely persecuted, if at all. They made up stories later about earlier persecution in order to make their heroes from the past look good, and after Constantine they made up even more stories about martyrdom in order to control people and oppress those who had different beliefs.

Both of these positions contain a kernel of truth but are overall very misleading. In response to the first theory, yes, there were times and places in which Christians had to hide. But most persecution in the first few centuries was sporadic and localized and not empire-wide until at least the middle of the third century (more on that in the section on Cyprian).

In response to the second theory, yes, after Constantine there were bishops who apparently made up the names of some martyrs and stories about them in order to increase control of churches or gain certain political advantages. But the suggestion that all stories of persecution were made up is simply false. Many Christians really died, as the evidence from that time proves.

Outside the New Testament, our earliest and best evidence for persecution and martyrdom comes from Roman sources, not Christian ones. Allow me to repeat that: *Our earliest and best evidence for persecution and martyrdom comes from Roman sources, not Christian ones.* Why does this matter? It matters because those who claim that Christians were not persecuted must argue that these Roman historians—who were often strongly anti-Christian—either did not know what they were talking about or did not mean to say what they clearly said about the fate of Christians.

Christians were persecuted, but it was mainly local. Even the early imperial persecutions seem to be primarily local. To demonstrate this, let us look at perhaps the most famous early imperial persecution.

The year was 64 CE, and Nero sat on the throne of the Roman Empire. The Roman sources agree that he was feared and hated by nearly everyone because he had become increasingly paranoid, violent, unpredictable, and self-absorbed. He was famous for sexual perversion and all kinds of other horrific actions, including the murder of his mother and his first wife, both of whom were popular among the Roman people.

Nero now set his eyes on building a new palace in the center of Rome, his Golden House (as it came to be known). There was a problem, however: many people already lived where he wanted to build. On the night of July 18, a large fire broke out in that very neighborhood and burned for nine days, destroying over half of the city. The ground for Nero's new house was now clear.

Almost immediately, the Roman people were suspicious of the emperor, and soon the word on the street was that Nero had set the fire on purpose. Now I will tell you something shocking. Ancient politicians did not always

Photo by Dr. Steve Kershaw

Figure 2.1 Person condemned to the wild beasts (El Djem). Perpetua and the others would have died in a similar setting.

take responsibility for their actions, and ancient politicians sometimes tried
to blame other people for things they had done.

Nero employed both strategies. First of all, he put on a big show of making
sacrifices to the gods to ask for their help after this great tragedy. *Oh gods,
how could this happen to us?* Second, he tried to bribe people to be quiet.
But when those strategies did not work, he had a backup plan. He needed a
scapegoat to shift the blame from himself, so he looked for an easy target.

The Christians were the perfect people for the job. Many people did not
know much about them, except perhaps that they were a new religious sect
somehow associated with Judaism. Many people in the Roman world thought
the Jewish people were uncultured barbarians (because of their circumcision
practices and food laws), so Christians probably posed a threat on some level.
Nero therefore blamed the Christian traitors for setting the fire.

All this was described for us by the Roman historian Tacitus, who wrote
a history of the early Roman emperors called the *Annals*. In his section on
Nero, he recounted the story and its aftermath. The account is worth quoting at length:

> But all human effort, all the lavish gifts of the emperor, and all the offerings
> to the gods did not subdue the sinister belief that the fire was the result of an
> order. Therefore, to get rid of this report, Nero fastened the guilt and inflicted
> the most exquisite tortures on a class hated for their abominations, called
> Christians by the people. Christus, from whom the name had its origin, suf-
> fered the extreme penalty during the reign of Tiberius at the hands of one of
> our governors, Pontius Pilate. But a most mischievous superstition, although
> halted for the moment, again broke out not only in Judea, the first source of
> the evil, but even in Rome, where all things hideous and shameful from every
> part of the world find their center and become popular. Thus, all who pleaded
> guilty [of being Christian] were arrested. Then, based upon their information,
> an immense multitude was convicted, not so much of the crime of setting the
> city on fire, but of hatred against humankind. Mockery of every sort was added
> to their deaths. Covered with the skins of beasts, they were torn by dogs and
> perished, or were nailed to crosses, or were doomed to the flames and burned
> alive to serve as lighting after the sun had gone down. Nero offered his own
> gardens for the spectacle. (*Annals* 15.44)

Distractions and bribes were not working, so Nero blamed the Christians of
the city and began to murder them for public entertainment. Their deaths
took place in the arena (probably the Circus Maximus) and along the streets.
 Nero was trying to show the Romans what he did to Rome's enemies—even
though the Christians were not Rome's enemies.

Tacitus states that the Christians were framed for the fire, but he still despised them because of their "hatred against humankind." Why hatred? Because they refused to take part in traditional Roman religious practices, and therefore they put everyone at risk.

This Roman historian who says that Nero unfairly framed and tortured the Christians also hated Christians. He was no Christian apologist, and he had no interest in furthering their cause, so he had no reason to make up a story about persecution. *When someone who hates you says that you are being treated unfairly, that is a good indication that you are in fact being treated unfairly.* This was the situation with Tacitus describing the torture and death of Christians for a crime they did not commit.

As a footnote to this conversation, Christian tradition states that Peter and Paul died during the reign of Nero. Neither death was directly tied to the fire in the sources, but their martyrdom stories clearly paint the reign of Nero as a dangerous time for Christians.

Other outbreaks of persecution seem to come out of nowhere: Antioch in Syria and the Black Sea region in the early second century; Smyrna in the middle of the second century; and Africa and Lyons (France) in the late second century, to name a few. Often the sources do not tell us why persecution broke out in the first place. Maybe it was not even clear to them at the time what triggered the persecution, apart from general suspicion and mistrust. This is why the work of the second-century apologists was primarily to destroy the myths that could lead to violent action against Christians.

Understanding Context

What, then, does all this mean for the historical context of early Christianity? It means that for early Christians, persecution might happen at any time and in any place. There did not need to be a big event to spark it, because many people in the Roman Empire already hated Christians and saw them as a danger.

In the next two chapters we are going to examine the story of two young women who were swept up in a persecution in Carthage in the year 202 or 203 CE. Their only "crime" was being a Christian. But that was enough to earn them death.

3

Perpetua and Felicity

Models of Christian Devotion

─────────────────── **Key Ideas** ───────────────────

- Perpetua and Felicity were young mothers who died because they refused to deny their faith.
- These two women took literally the words of Jesus when he said that faith is more important than family.
- Perpetua and Felicity were models of Christian discipleship because they valued their faith more than their own lives.

The *Passion* (literally, *Suffering*) *of Perpetua and Felicity* is one of the most famous of all martyr stories. It tells us some important information about Christian values in this period, and in the next chapter we will look at some of the questions it raised.

The Heroines

The story of Perpetua and Felicity is about two young women killed in Carthage around 202 or 203 CE. What is special about this text and has made it so popular and beloved throughout all of Christian history is that it includes a lengthy eyewitness account. We have the words of Perpetua herself talking about her own experiences leading up to death.

What caused her to come to the point of martyrdom? What was she thinking about as she was preparing for martyrdom? What were the challenges she
faced in terms of martyrdom? What was at stake for her? In Perpetua we have
a personal story about what this young woman was putting on the line and
giving up for the sake of her faith.

We begin by looking briefly at Perpetua, the main character and heroine
of the story. What do we know about her? From the text we learn two key
things about her background.

First, Perpetua was from the upper class and was well educated. The text
describes her as being from the nobility, and the fact that Perpetua wrote so
much of this account is confirmation of this. In a period when the literacy
rate was very low, having the ability to write was unusual. It would have been
particularly unusual for a woman in that time.

Some scholars estimate the literacy rate in the ancient world at around
ten percent. Of those ten percent, how many of them were women? That

Figure 3.1 Mosaic image of Perpetua (Ravenna)

number was very small for cultural reasons. Women were not expected to go into public life, so they were not educated in the same way men were. With few exceptions, women could not have prominent political careers, so literacy education was not seen as necessary. Perpetua was therefore from an unusually privileged situation.

We also read later in the text that she could speak more than one language. In a vision given to another martyr, Perpetua spoke with a bishop and an elder in Greek. The fact that she spoke both Latin and Greek also suggests a high level of education.

She came from the aristocracy. She had a comfortable, wealthy life. She was an educated woman. In other words, she had a lot to lose by standing up for her faith.

Second, Perpetua was a young wife and mother. The text states that she was still nursing her infant son and that she died at the age of twenty-two. When I teach this text to college students, I remind the seniors that she was their age. She was not wrestling with career choices or her social media presence. She was facing a life-and-death decision that involved not just herself but also her baby. She even says that her child became sickly while she was in prison. She was a young mother, her baby was at risk, and she was presumably walking away from a young husband. In other words (again), she had a lot to lose by standing up for her faith.

Let me pause for a moment to address an issue that sometimes comes up concerning this text. As is true with many texts from early Christianity, there are people who read the *Passion of Perpetua and Felicity* with great cynicism and suspicion. You may find someone on the internet or in a book claiming that this entire story was made up. *Of course, a woman would not have written this down. Women could not read and write. This was not an eyewitness account. It was someone later making up a story to sound like an eyewitness account and make Christians look better.*

That view is out there, but the text gives us no reason to doubt the identity or authenticity of the author. It is possible that an aristocratic woman would have known how to read and write, and even the earliest readers of this text (the ones most likely to know if it was fake) accepted it as Perpetua's words. The main reason that some read this text and doubt its legitimacy is because they want to doubt it. They come to the text with suspicion, and then they project their own assumptions onto the text. But to this point no one has raised any solid arguments against this being the true words of Perpetua. And despite what some may think, skepticism alone is not an argument.

For most of history, historians—Christian and not—have looked at this text as an eyewitness account of a soon-to-be martyr. Most scholars today still agree that this is the case, and I share the position that we are looking through the eyes of a woman facing death at the beginning of the third century.

We know a lot less about the other main character, Felicity, who appears rather late in the story. We know that she was a pregnant slave and eventually gave birth. Part of the text says that the law did not permit a pregnant woman to be killed. She eventually gave birth and was glad that she could now be martyred. This way of thinking may seem strange to us, but this is how the situation is presented in the text.

Ultimately, what comes down to us is the story of two young mothers—one with a baby who is nursing, and another with a newborn baby. Both have a lot to lose, and both willingly go to their deaths for their faith.

The Story of Perpetua and Felicity

The account opens with a preface in which the story is described as a new example of the supernatural power of God (more on that in the next chapter). Then Perpetua along with some other catechumens (people preparing for baptism) are arrested.

Perpetua's father pleads with her multiple times to consider her family, especially him and the baby, and renounce her faith so that she may live. She refuses and while in prison she is baptized and has a vision telling her that she will face a martyr's violent death. In fact, Perpetua has a series of visions throughout the story. The next is of her brother, Dinocrates, who had died at the age of seven of a deforming cancer on his face. She sees him in a dream suffering and begins praying for him every night. She finally has another vision of him healthy and restored in the afterlife.

After another visit from her father, Perpetua dreams of a martyred deacon who is dressed in a white robe (cf. Rev. 6:11; 7:9–14) and calling her to join the other martyrs. Suddenly she is in the arena awaiting the wild beasts. But beasts do not come. Instead, an enormous Egyptian appears to face her in hand-to-hand combat. Before the combat begins, she is stripped bare to be oiled up, as was typical in ancient wrestling. But her female modesty is supernaturally (and strangely) protected, because she is changed into a man for the battle. She defeats the Egyptian and after waking up realizes that this battle represents her own coming battle against the devil.

Perpetua recounts one more vision, although this one is had by someone named Saturus. He sees himself alongside Perpetua being carried by four angels into heaven, where they see the scene of the worship of the Son of Man from Revelation 1:14–16. It is a vision of where they will soon go in reality.

Felicity is then introduced. She cannot join her companions in the arena because she is pregnant. The others pray for her to give birth early, and God answers their prayers. Felicity gives birth to a little girl, and another Christian woman takes the child to raise as her own. The martyrs-to-be enjoy a final meal under the watchful eyes of curious onlookers, and Saturus warns the nonbelievers that they will see one another again on judgment day.

On the next day, they all enter the amphitheater with joy to face their fates—Felicity to face her "second baptism," this one in blood. Various wild beasts are let loose on the Christians, and some die in this way. Others survive the beasts and finally die by the sword. As for Perpetua, her young executioner is hesitant about dealing the death blow, so she guides his sword to her own throat and is killed.

A short postlude restates the importance of this story as an example that should strengthen and encourage the church.

Perpetua as a Model of Discipleship

This text introduces a number of themes that give us some insight into early Christianity. Some of these themes were received positively and will be the focus of the remainder of this chapter. But other themes were more controversial, and I will discuss those in the next chapter.

Faith over Family

One of the most startling of Jesus's statements is found in Luke 14:26: "If anyone comes to me and does not hate father and mother, wife and children, brothers and sisters—yes, even their own life—such a person cannot be my disciple." Does Jesus really want us to *hate* our biological family?

Matthew 10:34–37 can be equally jarring: "Do not suppose that I have come to bring peace to the earth. I have not come to bring peace, but a sword. For I have come to turn 'a man against his father, a daughter against her mother, a daughter-in-law against her mother-in-law—a man's enemies will be the members of his own household.' Anyone who loves their father or mother more than me is not worthy of me; anyone who loves their son or daughter more than me is not worthy of me." Son against father? Daughter against mother? (Of course, comedians make a living off daughter-in-law against mother-in-law jokes.)

These are strong statements, but in both cases Jesus makes it clear that he is not against the biological family. Rather, he demands that our allegiance to him surpass everything else. This is clear in Luke if we read the next verse: "And whoever does not carry their cross and follow me cannot be my disciple"

(14:27). Matthew's account gives the same follow-up message: "Whoever does not take up their cross and follow me is not worthy of me. Whoever finds their life will lose it, and whoever loses their life for my sake will find it" (10:38–39).

O Jesus calls for radical commitment that puts the family of God ahead of our human family. Nothing less will do.

Perpetua models this type of commitment in the text. In doing so she challenges the reader and displays blatant rejection of what in that time were considered "traditional family values." Like today, the Roman world also had traditional family values.

Roman families were led by the father of the family, the *paterfamilias*. He had authority over his wife, his children, and the household servants/slaves. This authority was complete and unquestioned. (As a side note, this means that the teachings about household organization in Eph. 5–6 and Col. 3 were radical in their own time because they demanded something of the husband/father/master. He had a responsibility to be fair, kind, and loving. These passages might seem "traditional" today, but they did not line up with the Roman way of thinking. Ephesians and Colossians put the *paterfamilias* under another, higher authority, so he could not do whatever he wanted.)

o By traditional Roman standards, Perpetua's primary responsibilities were to the most important relationships in her life: her father, her husband, and her child. In this text, she violates all those expectations. The primary relationships featured are her father and her son (the husband is strangely absent from the story). The father does a lot of talking and persuading. He says to her,

> Have pity on my gray hairs, daughter. . . . Have pity on your father—if I am worthy to be called your father. With my own hands I tended you like a blossoming flower. I favored you over both your brothers. So don't cast me aside now to be scorned by men! Think of your brothers . . . your mother . . . your aunt . . . your son! He won't be able to live without you. Don't be so stubborn, or you're going to destroy us all! (*Pass. Perp.* 5)[1]

Notice what he does here to try to persuade her. He tells her plainly: *Perpetua think about me; I am your father. Think about your mother. Think about your family. Think about your child. How can you go against the traditional values? Do not put your faith in front of your family, because if you do that,*

---

1. Translations from *Passion of Perpetua and Felicity* are taken from Bryan M. Litfin, *Early Christian Martyr Stories: An Evangelical Introduction with New Translations* (Grand Rapids: Baker Academic, 2014), 93–109.

all of us are going to suffer. In fact, he says at one point that the baby will die without her.

Her father's concern for his own well-being is not misplaced. At one point in the story Perpetua again refuses to renounce her faith, and the governor has her poor father beaten for this outrage, not her. She feels sorry for her father, who has to suffer the direct consequences of her choices.

The father is not done yet, however. Perpetua and company appear again before the governor, and her father shows up with heavy ammunition: "Everyone with me [Perpetua] confessed their faith when asked. Then it was my turn. At that point my father appeared there with my baby boy." At the moment when Perpetua is being asked to confirm her faith, and thus condemn herself to death, her father shows up holding her infant son in his arms. He begs her to offer the pinch of incense on behalf of the emperor. It was a simple action that would have saved her life and her son: "Perform the sacrifice! Have pity on your baby!" (*Pass. Perp.* 6).

Even Hilarian the Roman governor gets involved trying to convince her. He says, "Spare your gray-haired father! Spare your infant son! Just make a sacrifice for the emperor's well-being" (*Pass. Perp.* 6). He honestly may not have wanted to see this young mother massacred either. Remember that he probably did not care at all what she believed. He just needed to do his duty of making her sacrifice. But she refused to budge.

It can be easy for us to read this and move on, but if we think about it, this is a very emotionally charged scene. At this moment, Perpetua is deciding between her faith and her family. Her infant son is right there in front of her. Would it be too much to imagine that the baby is reaching out for his mother?

Perpetua, however, is unmoved. She effectively says, *My faith is more important than these traditional family values, and I will follow God at all cost—and trust God to keep my baby alive.* Felicity, who has just given birth to her baby, makes the same choice. If we are honest, this is a disturbing scene, for it also grates against modern cultural values about motherhood.

The text forces the audience (including us) to think hard about the overall cost of persecution. What are Christians giving up when they die? In the ancient period, like today, when we hear stories of Christians dying, we have to remember that whole families are being affected. Whole generations of families are being affected by this. The death of one Christian is never just the death of one Christian. There are always families and communities involved who also are suffering when martyrdom happens.

Jesus said, "Anyone who loves their father or mother more than me is not worthy of me; anyone who loves their son or daughter more than me is not worthy of me" (Matt. 10:37). Perpetua lived out that greater love for Jesus.

Faith over Life

We often think of martyrdom as choosing *faith* over *life*—being willing to give up your own life. Perpetua had already shown her willingness to put faith over family, but Jesus also said, "If anyone comes to me and does not hate father and mother, wife and children, brothers and sisters—yes, even their own life—such a person cannot be my disciple" (Luke 14:26). Perpetua follows this through to completion and chooses her faith over her survival. She thinks about this theologically, taking the eternal view over the human view. She thinks about eternal survival, not just survival in this life.

The Roman governor Hilarian gives her one last chance to save herself. He asks her the question with which she will save or condemn herself: "Are you a Christian?" This question shows up in a number of martyrdom texts, and Perpetua gives the martyr's answer: "I am a Christian." She writes, "Hilarian sentenced us all to face the wild beasts. Rejoicing, we went down into the dungeon" (*Pass. Perp.* 6). Like many figures in other stories from Africa and elsewhere, Perpetua stated, "I am a Christian," knowing that this would seal her fate. Her response to the death sentence was not sadness or fear but joy.

Those who are not Christians (and maybe even some who are) may read texts like this and think that something was wrong with Perpetua. Had she lost her senses? What would cause her to do this? Was this not basically committing suicide for no reason?

But within the Christian tradition we understand that Christ says, "Lay down your life." In the relative comfort and safety of the Western world, we tend to read this metaphorically: *Put faith ahead of my career. Put faith ahead of pursuing wealth and power*. Those are not bad instincts.

But we know that historically and still in many parts of the world today Christians literally lay down their lives—their physical lives.

Perpetua and Felicity chose to do this. In doing so, as the preface states, they provide an example for others to follow and encouragement for others facing the fires of persecution.

4

Perpetua

Leadership and Controversy

┌─────────────────── *Key Ideas* ───────────────────┐

- The controversial New Prophecy movement (Montanism) spread in the late second century and may have impacted the story of Perpetua and Felicity.
- The emphasis on divine guidance through visions in the *Passion of Perpetua and Felicity* upset some because it suggested an authority structure outside the official structure of the church.
- The story of Perpetua was also problematic for some in that women were featured as authoritative figures.

As we saw in the preceding chapter, the *Passion of Perpetua and Felicity* was a popular text that was presented as an example of Christian behavior. The main characters in the story lived out very literally the words of Jesus and his call for discipleship. True discipleship means putting the kingdom first, even ahead of our families and our lives. These factors have contributed to the ongoing popularity of the text for over eighteen hundred years.

However, not all aspects of the text were as uncontentious as the call to obedient discipleship. There were also elements of the text that caused controversy in their time, for they potentially threatened the power of some church officials and were seen as theologically dangerous.

The Rise of the New Prophecy

In order to understand this better, we need to go back a few years in church history and visit a different part of the Mediterranean. Sometime between 150 and 170 CE, a movement arose within Christianity in the region of Phrygia in Asia Minor (the western part of modern Turkey). It was led by Montanus, a man who believed that he was receiving revelations from the Holy Spirit. Some called the movement Montanism from the name of its founder, or Cataphrygianism ("the movement from Phrygia"), but they called themselves the New Prophecy.

It is difficult to reconstruct a detailed history of the movement because many sources are lost or overtly biased, and some were intentionally destroyed by opponents within Christianity. But we can understand some of the prominent features of the New Prophecy.

As the name might indicate, the group placed a strong emphasis on direct revelation from the Holy Spirit. The leaders believed that they were receiving ecstatic visions like the one described by the apostle Paul in 2 Corinthians 12. God was giving them direct insight into the present and the future, and they spread the message through the words they spoke under the Spirit's direction. This was special grace, *charisma*, given to them by God.

Figure 4.1 Montanist holy city of Pepouza

Photo by William Tabbernee

They believed that the new Jerusalem coming down from heaven in Revelation 21 was going to be a physical place on earth. In fact, on a large plain between their two holiest cities, Pepouza and Tymion, they identified the place where the new Jerusalem would descend.

But there was more. Because their prophets were receiving visions directly from the Holy Spirit, they did not need to yield to the authority of any other church officials, including bishops. Spiritual authority was given to anyone whom the Holy Spirit chose to receive such visions. This spiritual authority did not require ordination or recognition by any human authority, at least not in the minds of proponents of the New Prophecy.

By the time the New Prophecy came onto the scene, the church across the Mediterranean world was already appealing to the notion of apostolic succession. A bishop had authority because he had been ordained by another bishop who could in turn trace his line of ordination all the way back to the apostles. This line of succession identified bishops as the source and guarantee of true teaching and of continuity with the New Testament church, but the New Prophecy challenged this. Prophets inspired by God were the true successors to the apostles. Inspiration, not pedigree, was the mark of continuity.

On top of that, two women, Priscilla and Maximilla, joined Montanus as the leaders of the group. These women also claimed to receive prophetic messages from God. In an era when women did not hold many positions of authority in the church, this was another controversial aspect of the movement.

Finally, the New Prophecy emphasized asceticism, the denial of the physical desires and even needs of the body as a spiritual discipline. Sexuality was therefore a sign of spiritual inferiority, even within marriage. Martyrdom, however, was the ultimate example of self-denial for the sake of the gospel.

Opponents of the movement made other claims—particularly adversaries looking back in later centuries—that were even more extreme and cannot be confirmed. Some accused Montanus of claiming that he himself was the Holy Spirit. Some said he was a converted pagan priest of the god Apollo and had brought his pagan practices into Christianity. The sanctuary of Apollo at Delphi in Greece was a source of oracles through a female priestess called the Pythia. Opponents of the New Prophecy claimed that Montanus had just reproduced this practice through his two female companions, thereby accusing Priscilla and Maximilla of being pagan priestesses posing as Christians. Some even said that the spirit that inspired the New Prophets was the spirit of Satan, not the Holy Spirit.

Despite the objections to the movement, it spread rapidly. By the year 200 CE, its popularity had reached Rome, where some church officials soon felt the need to counter it (more on that in chap. 7). It also spread to Africa by 202/203 CE, the time of Perpetua and Felicity. Authors at the time, even critics, typically presented Montanism more as a schism (a division from the majority church) than a heresy (a movement that teaches ideas in direct conflict with the gospel).

Christian attempts to suppress the New Prophecy continued for several centuries, and eventually Montanism came to be treated more like a full-blown heresy. Around 230 CE a group of church leaders in eastern Phrygia declared that Montanist baptisms were invalid, so those wanting to join the majority church had to be rebaptized. Constantine ordered the destruction of Montanist writings in the early fourth century, and in 381 the Council of Constantinople declared that Montanists should be viewed as unbelievers. If they came forward to join the majority church, they had to be put through a process of catechism (training before baptism), exorcized (presumably from evil spirits), and then rebaptized.

As late as the sixth century, the emperor Justinian demolished some remaining Montanist churches. In 549 or 550, John, a bishop of Ephesus, found bones believed to be those of Montanus, Maximilla, and Priscilla. He burned their remains, thus punishing them like heretics.

In the eyes of some later authors, this divisive or possibly heretical movement had been properly eliminated. Authority returned to the proper place: the bishops who were part of the approved church hierarchy. They were the source of *orthodoxy* ("correct teaching") and the link to divine truth, not a group of upstarts from a backwater part of the world who claimed to hear directly from God.

The New Prophecy and Perpetua?

Now that we know a bit more about the historical context of Perpetua and Felicity's time, particularly with reference to the New Prophecy movement, we can return to the text and see more than we perhaps noticed before. I will suggest that the text reveals three potential sources of controversy, all connected to one another and to the New Prophecy movement.

Direct Visions from God as the Primary Source of Guidance and Authority

Throughout the text, the characters look to revelations in the form of dreams and visions.

As mentioned in the preceding chapter, a preface was added to the text, so we in fact read this preface before we begin reading the words of Perpetua.

The author of the preface wants the reader to interpret the entire text with several important themes in mind. In the preceding chapter we looked at one of these themes: model Christian behavior in the face of persecution. Now we will examine the preface more completely.

The importance of prophecy is another theme of the preface. The author recognizes that some may see contemporary examples of charismatic power as being inferior to ancient ones, but this should not be the case. The power of God was as great as ever, and the works of the Holy Spirit were as profound as anything God had ever done. The author paraphrases Acts 2:17, which is itself an echo of Joel 2:28: "In the last days, God says, I will pour out my Spirit on all people. Your sons and daughters will prophesy, your young men will see visions, your old men will dream dreams."

Perpetua and company are living in those "last days," so their lives are evidence of this pouring out of the Spirit. This gives their story great importance: "We who recognize and respect not only these new prophecies but new visions too as being equally promised to us—we likewise consider all the other powers of the Holy Spirit as a provision for the church. This same Spirit was sent to administer all his gifts to everyone, according to the way the Lord distributed them to each person" (*Pass. Perp.* preface).

With an allusion to Paul's teaching that the Spirit gives all spiritual gifts (1 Cor. 12:11; cf. Rom. 12:6), the author highlights the ongoing work of the Spirit. This work includes "not only these new prophecies but new visions too." Some scholars read this as a reference to the New Prophecy movement. If this is correct, then the author of the preface wants readers to view the entire story of Perpetua through that lens. The story of Perpetua in some way should support and promote the beliefs and practices of the Montanists, and it does so in several key ways.

Visions play a significant role throughout this story. A vision in prison shows Perpetua that she is about to die a martyr's death, not escape punishment. In the midst of a time of prayer, her dead brother comes to mind, and she begins to pray for him. That night in a dream she sees him suffering, yet after several days of intense prayer on his behalf she has another vision of him relieved and joyful. Her impending battle with Satan is shown to her in a dream about a battle with an Egyptian gladiator. Finally, one of the other martyrs, Saturus, has a vision of the two of them being carried into heaven by four angels. The Holy Spirit therefore reveals all the important plot points of the story to the martyrs through visions.

While the visions are front and center, what is absent is also notable: Scripture.

Apart from the paraphrase of Acts 2 and the allusion to Pauline theology in the preface, there are no other scriptural references anywhere in the text.

This is not to suggest that Scripture was unimportant to these Christians, but it was not a prominent feature. This was different from other martyrdom accounts, which typically include a number of allusions to Scripture. Many present the suffering of the martyrs as imitations of the story of Jesus (e.g., *Acts of Peter* and *Acts of Paul*) and/or the apostles (e.g., *Martyrdom of Poly-carp* and *Acts of Cyprian*), but there is none of that here.

The Holy Spirit, through direct revelation, is the source of authority. There is no need for anything else to stand between the martyrs and God. This idea fits well with the beliefs of the New Prophecy movement.

Spiritual Authority Distributed among Many People

Because the Spirit can reveal things directly to anyone, anyone can act and speak on God's behalf. In the context of the *Passion of Perpetua and Felicity* more specifically, this means that all the spiritual power does not belong to the ordained clergy. In fact, in this text most of it does not.

Perpetua mentions two deacons, Tertius and Pomponius, who were minis-tering to the soon-to-be martyrs while they were in prison. Pomponius serves as a messenger between Perpetua and her father, and in one of her visions he stands with her in the arena—but as her equal, not her superior. Presumably, one of these deacons baptizes Perpetua when she is in prison, but this is never described. This act of clerical authority over her is simply left out of the story.

Only one bishop appears in the account. A certain Optatus, perhaps the bishop of Carthage, shows up late in the text in Saturus's vision, yet he is in the vision because he is in trouble. He is in conflict with a presbyter (elder) named Aspasius, who is a "teacher" in the local church. The bishop and the elder ask the soon-to-be martyrs to help resolve their dispute: "They threw themselves at our feet and urged, 'Reconcile us! For you've gone away and left us in a state of division'" (*Pass. Perp.* 4). The vision does not reveal the specific source of the controversy, but this does not impact the dramatic na-ture of the scene. Instead of the recently baptized Perpetua and the layman Saturus bowing before the bishop, the bishop and the elder fall at their feet to beg for assistance.

The meaning is clear: Perpetua and Saturus, about to be martyrs, exercise spiritual authority over members of the church hierarchy because they have the power of the Holy Spirit. This does not, however, change the surprise that the martyrs feel in the situation: "Aren't you our bishop and our presbyter? How can *you* cast yourselves at *our* feet?" The martyrs then bend down to the level of the bishop and the elder, and Perpetua begins to speak with them. The power resides with her, for she lowers herself to their level.

Then the angels, clearly irritated, tell Optatus and Aspasius to leave the martyrs alone and go work out their differences on their own. They drive them away and give Optatus a parting rebuke for not leading effectively. The people are unruly and divided over various controversies—like sports fans arguing over different teams (yes, the angels use this exact analogy)—and the fault rests with their bishop.

The martyrs are the reliable source of spiritual influence. The bishop and the elder are the ones causing and allowing division (schism), while the martyrs are the ones who can restore unity.

A brief statement attached to the end of the text restates this point. The martyrs are "supremely brave and blessed martyrs! Truly you have been called and chosen for the glory of our Lord Jesus Christ!" They are "exemplary stories for the edification of the church" and prove that "that one and the same Holy Spirit is always at work, even now" (*Pass. Perp.* 6). This text therefore challenges the official power structure and identifies those empowered by the Holy Spirit, whoever they might be, as having authority. Like the wind, the Spirit moves wherever it wishes (John 3:8).

Spreading of the Charisma Placed Women in Prominent Roles

Before we build on the theological issue raised in the point above, let us begin by restating a general cultural observation. This is a text from the ancient world that is primarily about women and in which a woman has the main voice, which was quite unusual in that period. Other texts with women as important characters existed, but a text with women in the leading roles was rare, and it was exceedingly rare to find anything written by a woman.

Other named martyrs also appear in this text. Some are even mentioned at the beginning: Revocatus, Saturninus, and Secundulus. The endings of their names (Latin *-us*) tells us that they are male. But they immediately fade into the background as minor characters, while the two women in the text's initial list (Perpetua and Felicity) move into the spotlight. Saturus (another male) and a few others show up later as companions of Perpetua, but they never upstage her. Even the bishop Optatus kneels before her.

At the end of the text we also discover that Perpetua is stronger and braver than her executioner. After the wild beasts fail to kill Perpetua, a gladiator is sent to finish the job with a sword. However, he lacks the courage to do the deed until Perpetua takes over: "Then she herself guided the young and inexperienced gladiator's wavering hand to her throat. Perhaps we might say that such a great woman, who was feared by the demon within the executioner, couldn't be killed unless she herself allowed it" (*Pass. Perp.* 6). This young woman, the mother of an infant, displays more courage in the arena than a trained killer does. Even the demon within her executioner is afraid of her. This certainly is a countercultural image in that time.

Now we come to the theological angle of the emphasis on female characters, particularly Perpetua. And this brings us back around to the New Prophecy question.

There are still lively debates about the interpretation of certain New Testament passages as they relate to the role of women in the church. I have no intention of diving into the middle of those modern debates, so I will speak only descriptively about what we know from this particular period of history. It appears from the evidence that in the time of Perpetua, at least, men typically held the positions of authority in the church. Again, I am not saying what should or should not happen in the church today, but if we fail to recognize the reality of Perpetua and Felicity's world, then we fail also to recognize the provocative message of this text.

Not only does the Spirit empower people other than a bishop or a presbyter; the Spirit empowers two young women, notably Perpetua. Remember that she is the primary actor in the attempted reconciliation scene involving Optatus and Aspasius. Saturus has the vision, but Perpetua is the one who speaks to them as they attempt to resolve their conflict. She displays charismatic authority.

This further suggests a possible connection to the New Prophecy movement, in which Priscilla and Maximilla claim to receive visions alongside Montanus. The Montanists believe that the Holy Spirit gives gifts in the present time as freely as at any time in the past, and the author of the text's preface emphasizes that spiritual gifts in the last days are given to everyone. *Everyone.* There is no distinction or hierarchy in Acts 2 or Joel 2 on the basis of age, sex, or social status. Perpetua is from the upper classes, while Felicity is a slave, yet the Holy Spirit empowers them both.

The Legacy of Perpetua and Felicity

We do not know what sparked the persecution of Christians in Africa at the beginning of the third century, but we do know a few of the victims. These martyrs boldly followed the words of Jesus about the cost of discipleship. They put their faith ahead of their families and their lives and went willingly to their deaths. For this they were held up as examples of courage and proof that the Holy Spirit was as active and as powerful as ever.

Their story also tells us a few other things about the church in Africa at this point. Not everyone had the same idea about how the church should be run or who should run it. There were people in named church offices that we recognize: bishop, elder, and deacon. But the martyrs represented a source of spiritual authority outside the church hierarchy. They were inspired directly by the Holy Spirit, so the Spirit was the one deciding who was in charge. The charisma (spiritual power) could be distributed to anyone, not just to ordained clergy. Perpetua and Felicity were singled out from a group of martyrs, showing that women could also possess this authority.

I have suggested that the text's discussion of authority is tied to the growth of the New Prophecy movement, which came to Africa from Asia Minor. Some scholars dispute this point, and some translations have even been altered to make the potential conflict with the ordained clergy less obvious. But we cannot ignore that, according to the text, the church leadership structure in Africa had a significant problem since some Christians in the community were arguing that the martyrs, not the bishops, possessed the power of the Spirit in a special way and were the ones who could and should restore order and unity.

As history teaches us, the question of whether religious authority should be based on church structure or charismatic power has never been resolved. This question comes up again in the time of the bishop Cyprian of Carthage, as we will see later in this book, and it lies at the heart of some divisions among Christians to this day.

In the time of Perpetua, this conflict was as vibrant as in any period.

Part 2

Tertullian

5

The Life and Times
of Tertullian

┌─────────────────── *Key Ideas* ───────────────────┐

- Tertullian was a highly educated convert to Christianity whose theological thinking was well ahead of its time.
- Tertullian was a defender of and possibly a member of the New Prophecy movement after it came to North Africa.
- Tertullian's writings show both the outward focus of an apologist and the inward focus of a theologian.

└──┘

Tertullian is one of the most important early Christian theologians, but many people know little or nothing about him. In this chapter we will explore his life and context, and then in the next two chapters we will learn more about his theology and his apologetics.

Tertullian lived from approximately 145–220 CE. He came from Carthage, but he was not born into a Christian family. He grew up during a period when Christianity was not legal. It was not constantly suppressed, as we have seen, but there were enough cases of violent persecution that Tertullian was aware of this reality. Even prior to Perpetua and Felicity, Christians were being killed in Carthage, so when Tertullian converted to Christianity, he understood the challenges and the risks.

Eusebius of Caesarea, a church historian writing in the early fourth century, describes Tertullian as "highly skilled in Roman law and a man of high standing" (*Hist. eccl.* 2.2.4). Elements of Tertullian's ways of thinking and arguing sound like the approach of a lawyer (more on that in chap. 7), so many scholars agree that his background was in law. One tradition states that his father was a high-ranking government official, in which case Tertullian would have had access to an elite education.

For reasons we do not know, Tertullian becomes a Christian. Historians estimate that this occurrs no later than 197 CE (only about five years before the deaths of Perpetua and Felicity). He subsequently marries a woman who is also a Christian. This signals a major departure from the previous course of his life, but that is how he understands faith to work: "Christians are made, not born," he once wrote (*Apol.* 18).

Tertullian's life is surrounded by other mysteries. Did he ever have an official, ordained position in the church? From the way he is identified in his own writings and the later writings about him (including Eusebius), we know he was not a bishop. He is simply called Tertullian, not "Tertullian of . . ." We can compare this designation to that of other famous Christian figures. Later in this book I will discuss Cyprian of Carthage and Augustine of Hippo, both of whom were bishops. Other important early Christian theologians included

Figure 5.1 Remains of a Christian basilica in Carthage (Damous el Karita)

Courtesy of Robin M. Jensen

Clement of Alexandria, Irenaeus of Lyons, Athanasius of Alexandria, and Ambrose of Milan, all of whom were bishops.

Was Tertullian ever a priest or presbyter? Some, judging by comments from other authors such as Jerome (*Vir. ill.* 53.4), speculate that he was, but there is no clear evidence either way. Perhaps he was an educated layperson with some leadership responsibility in the local church, a category we know existed in the African church at that time.

Tertullian is not called a saint either. Neither the Western church nor the Eastern church recognizes him as a saint. The apostle Paul uses the term "saint" to describe all believers (e.g., Rom. 1:7; 1 Cor. 1:2; 2 Cor. 1:1), but over time some began to apply the term only to certain believers, who were special because of their theological or institutional importance or perhaps because they died as a martyr. Tertullian apparently does not fit into any of these categories.

The reasons Tertullian was never elevated to sainthood are not entirely clear, but there are a few clues. I discuss these issues more in the following two chapters, so here I will offer only a few introductory thoughts. The Eastern, Greek-speaking churches either were unaware of Tertullian or chose to ignore his work, so he was no one special to them. This is unfortunate, because if they had read his work, he could have saved them a lot of time and trouble at the church councils. (Incidentally, we know that Tertullian knew Greek because he produced Greek versions of several of his works.)

As we will learn in chapter 7, the theological formula about Christ that the Greek church struggled to create, defend, and adapt between 325 and 381 (in the Nicene Creed) is remarkably similar to what Tertullian developed before 220 CE. Thus, the Greek church was more than a century behind Tertullian on some matters of theology, but his contributions have never been recognized in the East.

In the West the perception of Tertullian has been influenced by the fact that he criticized the church in Rome. In chapter 6 we will see that Tertullian may have even accused the Roman bishop at the time of being a heretic. Tertullian was no friend of Rome, and the Roman church never made him a saint. In fact, the early twentieth-century *Catholic Encyclopedia* accuses Tertullian of "writing more virulently against the Church than even against heathen and persecutors."[1]

Are his critiques of the Roman church the result of purely literary interactions or of time spent in Rome? Yet again, historians can only speculate.

1. J. Chapman, "Tertullian," in *The Catholic Encyclopedia* (New York: Appleton, 1912), 14:521.

Small clues in Tertullian's writings suggest that he may have been in Rome at some point. Perhaps his dislike of some elements of the Roman church comes from personal experience in the city. We do not know for sure. Unfortunately, Tertullian never tells us this part of his autobiography.

Tertullian the Montanist?

What made Tertullian so negative toward the church in Rome? One of the major theories is that Tertullian disliked Rome and its bishops because the Roman church opposed the New Prophecy, a movement that Tertullian himself belonged to in later life. We must say up front that this theory is open to debate, so this by no means is an open-and-shut case. (You might be realizing by now that many theories about early Christianity are open to debate, primarily because the sources we rely on were addressing the questions and issues of their time, not our time.) Sources you come across might talk about Tertullian "leaving the church" and joining the Montanists, but there was no church membership in those days—at least not in the way we think about it now.

Many Christians at the time saw the New Prophecy movement as part of the church, even if it differed slightly from other expressions. For example, Irenaeus, the bishop of Lyons and a champion of orthodox theology, defended the New Prophecy as a legitimate expression of Christianity. Irenaeus is known as one of the most important theologians in early Christianity. He battled heresies in the late second century and argued for the authority of nearly all the texts we have in the New Testament. (Some modern scholars argue that there was no single orthodoxy ["correct teaching"] in early Christianity. However, those scholars have to deal with Irenaeus.)

Similarly, Cyprian of Carthage, the most beloved and important bishop of the early African church, spoke of Tertullian in glowing terms in the middle of the third century. He showed no hesitation about Tertullian's orthodoxy or his connection to the New Prophecy.

So I do not think there was really any issue with Tertullian "leaving the church." However, his possible connection to the New Prophecy is worth considering because it may help us understand his theology better and may have led him, in fact, to be well ahead of his time in his theology of the Holy Spirit.

We should explore for a few moments the connection between Tertullian and the New Prophecy—and possibly even between Tertullian and the *Passion of Perpetua and Felicity*.

In chapter 4 we looked at the New Prophecy movement, whose adherents were called the Montanists. Their theology and practices were controversial because their leaders believed that their authority came from direct revelations from the Holy Spirit. Montanus, Priscilla, and Maximilla were not part of the established church hierarchy, and they did not think they needed to be. They understood their right to teach as coming directly from the Spirit, not from recognition by another human teacher. On top of that, Montanists had women teaching and leading, which was not popular with other Christians, and Montanists encouraged forms of asceticism (self-denial) that others found too extreme.

The New Prophecy was gaining momentum in North Africa at the very time Tertullian converted to Christianity, and apparently the rigor of Montanism attracted him. Tertullian expressed concern that others in the church were too lenient on moral issues. On the issue of remarriage, which he discusses in *On Monogamy* and *On Modesty*, he teaches that the new law of Christ does away with the provisions in the Old Testament for divorce. He rejects any notion of remarriage by a Christian, even if the first spouse has died. He argues that even some pagan women honor their dead husbands by remaining celibate, so Christians should be able to do the same. The only way one can be remarried is if the previous marriage ended before the person became a Christian. (Because a person is a new creation at conversion, they effectively start over when it comes to marriage.) Those who believe otherwise are guilty of adultery. His views on this differ from those held by many others, including leaders in the Roman church. The ascetic strictness of Montanism clearly appealed to Tertullian.

In some of his writings Tertullian explicitly mentions the New Prophecy and their visions. His most direct defense of the movement, a work called *On Ecstasy*, has not survived. Perhaps it was not preserved because of anti-Montanist feelings among many in the church. But other sources also reflect his pro-Montanist stance. In *On Fasting: Against the Carnal Believers*, Tertullian comes out with both guns blazing against lazy, undisciplined Christians. Not only do they remarry freely, but they also fail to fast. He explicitly ties remarriage to gluttony because both focus on indulging the desires of the flesh.

Even worse than that, Tertullian writes, his Christian opponents criticize those who follow scriptural commands about denying the flesh. This is the true heart of their criticism of the Montanists. These carnal Christians, he says,

cause controversy about the Paraclete.[2] This is why the New Prophecies are rejected. It is not that Montanus and Priscilla and Maximilla preach another

---

2. "Paraclete" (*parakletos*) is a Greek word that can be translated as "helper," "comforter," or "advocate." Jesus uses this word to describe the Holy Spirit several times in John's Gospel (14:16, 26; 15:26; 16:7).

God, or that they somehow disconnect Jesus Christ [from God], or that they undermine any teaching about our faith and hope. The problem is that they plainly
teach that one should fast more often than one should get married. (*Jejun.* 1)

The charges against the theology of the New Prophecy, Tertullian argues,
have no merit. They are trumped-up accusations designed to mask the real
motivation of the critics. These critics are weak in their spiritual disciplines,
so the dedication of the Montanists makes them look bad, as it should. These
self-indulgent pseudo-Christians react by trying to undercut the Montanists
however they can, even to the point of accusing the Montanists of being inspired by the spirit of Satan, not the Holy Spirit.

Tertullian responds with a probing question: "How is it possible that he
[the spirit of Satan] could convict people to actions worthy of our God and
commands them to be offered to none other than our God?" He then goes on
the attack against the critics: "Either you must argue that the devil works with
our God, or you must say that the Paraclete is Satan" (*Jejun.* 11). Clearly, no
one wants to say either of these things, so the accusation that the Montanists
are inspired by an unclean spirit must be cast aside. Tertullian closes his argument by circling back to the issue of self-restraint. The very same bishops
who accused the Montanists of heresy engage in "double shares" of meat
and drink. Thus they are guilty of gluttony and therefore in no position to
criticize anyone else on moral grounds.

In *On Fasting* and in several other texts, Tertullian defends the New Prophecy. In particular, he is angered by what he thinks are attacks not just on
Montanus and others but, more seriously, on the Holy Spirit. As the quota-
tion above states, in Tertullian's mind any assault on the New Prophecy is an
assault on God. The Holy Spirit through the prophets of the past and present
has the task of leading people to God. To say that the New Prophecy is leading people away from God is actually to say that the Holy Spirit is leading
people away from God.

Tertullian believed he was defending the honor of the Holy Spirit when he
defended the Montanists. The laziness and laxity of the critics showed that
they were in no position to judge others.

Earlier I mentioned a possible connection between Tertullian and Perpetua,
so I will finish this chapter with a historical footnote and teaser. As we saw in the
chapters on Perpetua, an anonymous editor added a theological introduction
and conclusion to the *Passion of Perpetua and Felicity*. These additions declare
that the martyrs were inspired by "new prophecies" and should be models
of self-denial for others. These sections do not have a named author, but one
theory suggests that they were penned by none other than Tertullian himself.

Tertullian as Apologist and Theologian

Tertullian is virtually unmatched in Christian history because he is one of the most important apologists of his time *and* one of its most important theologians.

In the next two chapters we will see him in both roles. But before we dive into those details, we will pause and consider the work of an apologist versus the role of a theologian. These roles require two different kinds of writing with different goals and approaches. For this discussion I borrow insights from the work of James Papandrea, who has written extensively on the development of early Christian theology.[3]

I briefly mentioned the apologists in chapter 2, and here we will return to them in more depth. Apologetics is still a subject of study at many Christian schools, colleges, and seminaries, so it is useful to know more about its ancient roots.

Apologists had an external audience in mind. They were not writing for Christians, at least not primarily. Christians may benefit from the writing and feel confirmed in their faith, but apologists were primarily telling non-Christians about Christianity.

One of the most important tasks for an apologist is to establish a connection with the audience, and this requires a certain way of speaking and the use of certain strategies. An apologist cannot be combative right off the bat. Instead, apologists first look for common ground or understanding, which they can then use as a starting point for conversation.

An apologist has to agree to play by the rules of the audience. Whatever they value is what the apologist must value, at least at the start. The apologist might hope to change some of the values, assumptions, and perspectives of the audience—to change the rules of the game, if you will—but this cannot happen at the outset. If the apologist offends the audience at the start, then the cause may be lost.

Consider the example of the apostle Paul when he goes to Athens in Acts 17:16–34. He does not go into the city and immediately begin teaching Christian theology. Instead, he first spends a lot of time observing the many temples and shrines for gods and goddesses. He looks for a point of connection, and he finds it in a shrine dedicated to an unknown God. He affirms the Athenians' religious devotion but then says that he can tell them about that unknown God. Paul takes what they have already accepted, and he attempts to turn that into an opportunity for evangelism.

3. See especially James L. Papandrea, *Reading the Early Church Fathers* (New York: Paulist Press, 2012).

In terms of the early Christian apologists, this often means appealing to philosophy to show the reasonableness of Christianity. A generation before Tertullian, an apologist named Justin (Justin Martyr) takes this exact approach. In *Against Trypho* he opens by talking about his past search for truth. He claims (and I am paraphrasing), *I tried all kinds of philosophies. I tried them all. Name a philosophy, and I tried it. I was looking for the highest truth, and only when I came to Christianity did I find the highest form of truth.* For Justin, philosophy is the road that brings him to the truth of God, which is ultimately higher than any philosophy, higher than any human wisdom.

His argument is simple. If his audience also values philosophy and truth (he assumes they do), then they will also come to believe in Christianity: "Reason directs those who are truly pious and philosophically informed to honor and love only the truth and to reject traditional beliefs if they are found to be worthless" (*1 Apol.* 2). The clear choice for his readers is to adopt the Christian philosophy.

To be honest, Tertullian finds it harder than Justin does to recognize much good in pagan philosophy. He appeals to the authority of Greek and Roman philosophy and literature that is assumed by his non-Christian audience, but then he turns it against itself. In his *Apology*, Tertullian attempts to show that pagan beliefs and practices contradict one another and that no one lives according to the teachings of their own philosophers and authors anyway. He chips away at the assumptions of his audience by trying to show that they are inconsistent, but he starts by engaging with ideas that they hold authoritative. He does not open with an attack, because he hopes to convince his audience to come around to his way of thinking. After he has weakened the pagan worldview, then he constructs the Christian alternative.

One final observation about apologists is important: they do not cite much Scripture because non-Christian readers do not know or care what it says. If Scripture has no authority for the audience, then quoting it will do nothing to advance the argument.

Theologians have a different task because they are writing for an internal audience, a Christian audience. They are usually trying to convince people not about Christianity as a whole but about certain beliefs or practices within Christianity. A theologian is trying to say that certain things are true about God or Christ or the Holy Spirit or that they are true about the church or about how the church should live in the world. This is an internal conversation.

Theologians frequently appeal to Scripture in making their arguments because they assume that their audience values the words of the Bible. For example, in Tertullian's work *On Fasting* he does not just say that Christians should fast. He gives example after example from the Bible, almost to the point of exhausting the reader. Why? Because he is trying to show that anyone who values Scripture must think the same way he does about this issue.

Many early Christian theologians tended to be skeptical of philosophy because philosophy was seen as a secular, even a pagan, way of thinking—trying to get to truth using human wisdom instead of appealing to divine wisdom. In fact, many early theologians, including Tertullian, warn that trying to mix philosophy with theology leads to heresy. When human reason is made to be the highest good and the ultimate standard for truth, then the teaching and conclusions will always miss the mark.

We will explore these ideas more in the next chapter.

Overall, Tertullian is a complex figure in a challenging setting. He has sometimes been accused of being too direct and aggressive, and perhaps he is at points, but we must keep in mind what is at stake for him. He is trying to explain and defend Christianity in a time when Christians (such as Perpetua) could be killed just for being Christians (see chap. 6). And he is caught up in debates within Christianity about fundamental theological ideas, including the nature of the Godhead and the person and work of the Holy Spirit (see chap. 7).

6

Tertullian Defending the Faith

Apologetics and Heretics

Key Ideas

- Tertullian presented logical arguments in his works, but he still maintained that reaching the highest truths about God could not be done through philosophy or human reasoning.
- As an apologist, Tertullian argued that Christianity reflected ancient and superior understanding, while pagan philosophy and religion were inferior and irrational.
- Writing as a theologian, Tertullian argued that attempts to reason our way to God through philosophy, instead of through Scripture, lead to heresy.

In the preceding chapter we looked at Tertullian the man, and I closed by discussing his work as both an apologist (writing for non-Christians) and a theologian (writing for Christians about Christian topics). Here we will see Tertullian in action in both roles through some of his writings.

The common thread in this chapter is Tertullian's distrust of philosophy. He is not anti-intellectual—quite the contrary. But he does not trust philosophy as the way to help a person find and understand the highest good and the highest truth. Tertullian's conviction that philosophy can never lead a person to ultimate truth informs his apologetic works and his writings against heretics.

If we reflect for a moment on our own context, we note that people still try to find their ultimate truth through some kind of philosophical system. The European Enlightenment gave rise to a "cult of reason," the idea that human wisdom and understanding can be the ultimate source of truth. The cult of reason says that because we cannot understand God through our rational minds, God cannot exist. Or even if God does exist, God certainly cannot know anything that we cannot know.

This belief appears, for example, in the Harvard University crest. Harvard was founded in 1636 to train clergy, and from 1643 to 1650 the crest featured a shield with three books. They had the Latin word *veritas* ("truth") written on them—*VE* on the first book, *RI* on the second book, and *TAS* on the third book. The first two books were open to the viewer, while the third book was turned face down, so *TAS* was actually on the back of the book. What were these three books? The first two represented the Old and New Testaments, the two "books" of truth that had been revealed by God. The third book could not be read, because it contained the truth known only to God, God's divine mysteries. Human beings could know some truth, but not all of it.

In 1847 Harvard changed its seal. Under the influence of the Enlightenment, the university concluded that no truth was available to God that could not also be accessed by humans, so the third book was turned over to be open to the viewer. The current Harvard seal features three open books. Human wisdom is the highest truth.

Tertullian would disagree with Harvard. If philosophy is your ultimate truth, he would say, you are misled and misguided. This is due to the corruption of human reason. Because we are fallen creatures, our reason is distorted and limited. How can a human being claim to have a full understanding of God? And how can a person claim to speak about the eternal affairs of God, to see things from God's perspective?

For finite beings, this is impossible. Reason is a human capacity, and Tertullian uses it in his writings, but it is always inferior to the thoughts of God and cannot ultimately lead us to God. For Tertullian, if we want to get to God, we have to go through the church. We cannot get to God directly through reasoning and philosophical speculations about God. If we want to understand God, if we want to have a relationship with God, we must go through the church. Why? Because the church has access to truth that is higher than any philosophy.

One of Tertullian's most famous questions is this: "What does Athens have to do with Jerusalem?" (*Praescr.* 7). Athens was the famous center of ancient Greek philosophy. It was home to the Academy, the philosophical school founded by Plato. Jerusalem was the center of life and faith for Judaism, and it was the starting point of Christianity, the place where Jesus died and rose again. Effectively, Tertullian is asking, "What does the center of Greek philosophy have to do with the center of our faith? What agreement is there between the academy and the church?"

For Tertullian, only the church, not the academy, can lead you to the greatest good. His suspicion of dependence on philosophy shows up in a number of his works, and we will look at two examples—one apologetic work (*Apology*) and one theological work (*Prescription against Heretics*).

Tertullian's *Apology*

We begin with Tertullian's *Apology*. As we saw in chapter 2, an ancient apology is an explanation or a defense, not a statement of regret, and this type of literature is not unique to Christianity. Plato wrote an *Apology* arguing that the teachings of Socrates were reasonable and not dangerous, and Tertullian wrote an *Apology* explaining and defending Christianity. Even today, Christian colleges and seminaries offer courses in apologetics, the study of how to explain Christianity and respond to critiques of it.

We are not sure what prompted Tertullian to write his *Apology* when he did, but one theory suggests that he wrote it after the death of Irenaeus of Lyons. Tertullian was a great admirer of the work of Irenaeus, a late-second-century bishop in Gaul (France) who spent much of his life preserving and protecting the core beliefs of the faith. One tradition suggests that Irenaeus may have died as a martyr. Perhaps, Tertullian thought, if even the noble Irenaeus could be killed for being a Christian, then someone needed to explain Christianity better to the outside world.

Although Tertullian rejects rational thought and philosophy as being the highest good, he still attempts to present a logical argument. But this does not mean that it is always a friendly argument. Modern contexts in which Christians use expressions such as "friendship evangelism" emphasize developing a positive personal relationship with a person before beginning to explain the Christian faith. Tertullian, however, is not remembered for being subtle or indirect. He could be abrasive and aggressive, perhaps the result of arguing legal cases in a courtroom.

In his *Apology* he does not pull any punches and makes a number of points. We will focus on four of these arguments.

First, Jerusalem is greater than Athens—the church is greater than the Academy—because it is older. The worship of God predates classical Greek philosophy. Here Tertullian appeals to a broader cultural idea that "older is better." While many companies today tend to market "new" or "new and improved" products, in the Roman world older was better.

We can see this in the Roman treatment of the Jewish population of the empire. Central to the survival of Rome, it was thought, was the worship of the traditional gods and goddesses. (We saw this above in chapter 2 on martyrdom.) "I give so that you give" was a Roman motto. Those who refused to worship the gods might anger them, and the gods in turn might punish the empire with plague, famine, or military defeat. The descendants of Abraham worshiped only one God and refused to worship the Roman gods. Others may have thought of Jewish religion as inferior and misguided, but they honored it—and the Romans allowed it to continue—because it was ancient.

Antiquity granted status and respect. In the *Apology*, Tertullian asserts that "our religion is supported by the writings of the Jews, the oldest that exist" (*Apol.* 21). He further argues that if there is anything good in pagan philosophy, it has come from the Scriptures, by which he means the Old Testament: "Which of your poets, which of your wise men have not drunk from the fountains of the prophets?" (*Apol.* 47). Moses and the other prophets are the source of any enlightened ideas of the philosophers.

But if non-Christians have misunderstood the Christian faith, it is because "the speculations of philosophers have perverted the older scriptures" (*Apol.* 47). The pagan philosophers may have stumbled onto some good, but they still manage to distort the truth. Tertullian effectively says, and I paraphrase, *Philosophy is new compared to the worship of the one true God, so it is inferior and can be misleading. You need to respect our faith as being rooted in something older and better, the Scriptures.*

Second, Tertullian argues that the polytheism of the Romans is foolish and illogical. According to Roman beliefs, the gods are supposed to protect those who honor them. But Tertullian cites numerous examples of cases in which the gods do not protect cities and regions from disaster, including destruction at the hands of the Roman Empire itself.

Tertullian then attacks the gods directly. Every old myth about the gods includes immoral behavior that would never be tolerated among humans. Zeus/Jupiter, for example, is a repeat sex offender and even mistreats a member of his own family, according to one myth. Also, the gods are always in such conflict with one another that if they were real, human society would never know peace. The Trojan War happens because of a divine battle based on petty jealousy and wounded pride. If the pagan gods were real, humans would forever be caught in these kinds of squabbles.

Even the pagan philosophers, who are corrupt in their thinking, attack and mock polytheism. Socrates mocks the stories of the Greek gods. He is killed for it, but then the Athenians realize their mistake and take revenge on his killers—thus showing that Socrates's critiques were correct in the first place. Tertullian cites other philosophers (the Greek Diogenes and the Roman Varro) who also ridicule the ignorance of polytheism (*Apol.* 14). In fact, in many cases the philosophers "openly overthrow your gods, and in their writings they attack your superstitions; and you applaud them for it" (*Apol.* 46). If even Greek and Roman philosophers see the foolishness of polytheism, how foolish it must be!

Tertullian continues his assault on the contradictions of paganism. How can there be different gods and goddesses with responsibility for the same city or activity? (There are multiple deities of war, for example.) Yet on the other hand, how can the same god have many different names in different places? (The sun god is called Helios among the Greeks and Sol among the Romans, but the god who drives the sun across the sky is Apollo.) And if the Greek system of gods is true, then what about the Egyptian system? They cannot both be true. The entire concept of polytheism, Tertullian asserts, does not make any sense. It is much more logical, he writes, to believe in one God over all things, not many inferior gods and goddesses constantly bickering with one another.

Third, wise Roman emperors treated Christians with fairness; on the contrary, wicked ones persecuted them. Tiberius, Trajan, Hadrian, and Marcus Aurelius were among those emperors who used their reason properly. They showed restraint toward the Christians and did not persecute them.

On the other hand, Nero and Domitian were "the most complete villains in impiety, injustice, filthiness, foolishness, and madness" (*Apol.* 5). Nero was the first to shed innocent Christian blood, and Domitian attempted to equal Nero's cruelty. Tertullian states that "the persecutors of Christians have always been men of this kind, with no sense of justice, piety, or shame" (*Apol.* 5). Even limited reason escaped them. Their evil was recognized by all, so much so that the Romans overturned many of their wicked laws.

The reader is therefore left with a question: Am I going to behave toward Christians as the good emperors did? Or am I going to mistreat them and be placed in the category of Nero, whose madness and wickedness were so great that his image and name were officially condemned by the Romans?[1] By presenting the argument in these terms, Tertullian is guiding the reader to say, "I want to be like Trajan." He is attempting to move the reader toward greater understanding and tolerance.

---

1. Even Roman sources agree that Nero was out of control, so much so that he suffered *damnatio memoriae* ("the condemnation of memory"). This was an official process that resulted in the removal of the emperor's name and likeness.

Fourth, Christians are model citizens of the empire. They pay their fair share of taxes to the state (apparently, in the ancient world, too, some people cheated on their taxes); they care for the poor; they are not thieves, sorcerers, or killers; and they are responsible parents to their children. It is true that they refuse to take part in pagan festivals, but they more than make up for that because they are a "defense against demons and are always on their knees praying to the true God on your behalf" (*Apol.* 13).

Thus, Tertullian presents four arguments: (1) philosophy cannot be trusted; (2) polytheism is irrational; (3) wise emperors are fair to Christians; and (4) Christians are the best citizens. With these arguments and many more like them, Tertullian attempts to make his case that the rational, logical way to live is not just to leave Christians in peace but is in fact to become one of them.

This is Tertullian's strategy as an apologist. This is how he writes when he is looking outward, explaining and defending Christianity to non-Christians.

Philosophy Leads to Heresy

The dangers of philosophy, for Tertullian, not only led to outsiders misunderstanding Christianity; they also led to distortion within Christianity itself—to heresy.

Courtesy of Robin M. Jensen

Figure 6.1 Roman amphitheater of Carthage

We see this clearly in a work called the *Prescription against the Heretics*. Tertullian asserts that the fundamental source of all heresy is philosophical speculation. Before giving his prescription, Tertullian first offers a diagnosis: philosophy is the cause of theological disease. Tertullian believes that the attempt to use human reason to comprehend divine mysteries leads people down the wrong path.

As he bluntly states, "Heresies themselves are caused by philosophy." He then goes into a lengthy attack on the teachings of Plato, the Stoics, the Epicureans, Aristotle, and others. Alluding to the Pauline letters, he condemns "the doctrines of men and of demons" (1 Tim. 4:1) that scratched the "itching ears [2 Tim. 4:3] of the spirit of the wisdom of this world" (*Praescr.* 7; cf. 1 Cor. 1:20; 3:19).

As these and other scriptural passages show, Paul warned against this. After the apostle visited Athens (see Acts 17:13–34) and became familiar with "that human wisdom that pretends to know the truth but only corrupts it," he warned his readers in multiple letters about the dangers of putting human wisdom above divine wisdom. In fact, in the Letter to the Colossians, Paul "expressly names philosophy as that which we must guard against" and warns the Colossians, "Be careful that no one takes [them] captive through empty and deceptive philosophy that depends on human tradition" (Col. 2:8) (*Praescr.* 7).

At the end of this passage Tertullian poses the famous question mentioned at the beginning of this chapter, which he ties directly to heresies: "What does Athens have to do with Jerusalem? What agreement is there between the Academy and the church? Between heretics and Christians?" (*Praescr.* 7).

Tertullian claims direct connections between ancient philosophers and the heretics of his own day, specifically Valentinus and Marcion. Valentinus represented Gnosticism, which was a mixture of elements of Christianity and obscure theories from Greek philosophy. Tertullian's critique focuses on Valentinus's complex theory about the existence of many spiritual beings not discussed in Scripture, and he blames Valentinus's outlandish theories on Plato's philosophy. Marcion argued for the existence of two gods: the evil god of the Old Testament, who created the world, and the good God of the New Testament, who lives only in the spiritual realm. Tertullian traces these ideas to the Stoics.

Tertullian thought that philosophy never stopped breeding heresy: "The same subjects are discussed over and over again by the heretics and the philosophers" (*Praescr.* 7). Since both philosophers and heretics relied on their own rational minds to answer questions about the nature of God (theology), the nature of humankind (anthropology), and the origin and nature of the universe (cosmology), they inevitably ignored and distorted the truth.

In *Prescription against the Heretics* Tertullian focuses on the ideas of philosophy as the roots of heresy more than on the heresies themselves. Yes, he highlights some examples of heresy, but these are not the main focus.

Notably, a later author was motivated to pick up and expand the work of Tertullian. There exists another text about heresy that for many years was also credited to Tertullian because it was copied into manuscripts that contained authentic writings of Tertullian. It is called *Against All the Heresies*. It includes a list of thirty-two different heresies, along with an explanation of the roots of each one. Valentinus and Marcion appear in this list, and they are accompanied by many others. Scholars have now established that Tertullian did not write this work, but the anonymous author clearly understood the intention of Tertullian's *Prescription* and decided to make sure that all the heretics of the time were called out by name.

Tertullian and Philosophy?

We may see a potential dilemma. How can Tertullian appeal to notions of reason from his Roman context and use examples of philosophers to make his argument in some of his writings, but then turn around and condemn those same ideas and philosophers as fatally flawed in other places?

The answer is that it depends on his audience and his goals. As an apologist, he has to find some common ground with nonbelievers—he must play by their rules at least to a certain extent. Eventually, he tries to show that pagan philosophy is flawed and foolish, but he cannot start at that point. A non-Christian audience would not have accepted divine truth as a category, so he must present Christianity in a way that makes sense to them. In his *Apology* he is trying to make an argument that will be logical from their point of view.

As a theologian, however, he assumes that his audience already agrees that divine wisdom trumps human wisdom. Philosophy and reason can never lead to ultimate truth. In fact, when Christians try to use philosophy to explain divine truths, they often fall into heresy. In his *Prescription* he tries to show how this happens.

So, does Tertullian think of philosophy and reason as fundamentally good or bad? To think about this question, let us consider a modern example of a similar question. Have you ever heard a pastor criticize sports for causing people to miss church but then turn around and use sports analogies in sermons? What is that pastor's true view on sports? Are sports fundamentally good or bad? You might say, *Well, it depends on the point they are trying to make.*

Exactly—and the same is true for Tertullian. Human reasoning is useful when it is useful (apologetics), and dangerous when it is dangerous (theology).

But God's divine wisdom revealed in Scripture remains the highest truth.

7

Tertullian Defining the Faith

The Fullness of the Trinity

┌──────────────── *Key Ideas* ────────────────┐

- Tertullian is recognized as the father of Latin theology, and he was the first to use the term "Trinity" in his writings.
- Tertullian wrote against Modalism, an early Christian heresy that denied the Trinity by collapsing the Father, the Son, and the Holy Spirit into one divine person wearing different masks.
- Tertullian explicitly stated that the Holy Spirit is God, but this was a matter of uncertainty in some parts of Christianity, including at the earliest church councils.

In this chapter we turn our attention again to Tertullian as a theologian and explore his role in explaining the doctrine of the Trinity.

I believe that Tertullian does not get enough credit for what he contributed to Christian theology, particularly on the Trinity. He was largely ignored in the Greek-speaking East because he wrote in Latin. All the church councils were held in Greek, so there was, perhaps, an assumption that anything important was said in Greek. Even in the Latin-speaking West, Tertullian was later overshadowed by Augustine. Augustine became the dominant theological voice in Latin, so Tertullian was largely forgotten by many people.

But ignoring Tertullian is a mistake, because he made significant contributions to Christian theology. He was another African whose effect on Christianity resounds even today.

We need to recognize that Tertullian has not always been popular. In his own time, he had conflicts with other Christians (more on this below), and modern readers have often seen him as overly strict. He was strong on sin, but then again, most ancient Christians took a more serious view of sin than modern Christians do. His views on the role of women are also not popular with many modern readers. I am not trying to convince you that you should agree with all his views. However, he made many important contributions, so he deserves to be studied and understood.

Scholars of Christianity refer to Tertullian as "the father of Latin theology" because he was the first writer to do serious theology in the Latin language. Irenaeus, his hero, wrote in Greek. So did Clement of Alexandria, another important theologian from Africa. But Tertullian was the first writer known to us to produce extensive theological works in Latin.

Tertullian also coined the term *trinitas*, from which we derive the English word "Trinity." While theologians have shown that the concept of the Trinity can be found in Scripture—Matthew 28:19 is the classic example—no author of Scripture named this theological idea. Tertullian did: *trinitas*.

Against Praxeas

We are going to focus on the work in which Tertullian addresses the Trinity most directly and completely: *Against Praxeas*.

We need to set up the context of this work before we look at the details. As is often the case with ancient situations, we do not have all the information we would like to have, but in this case we have enough information to make a good guess about why Tertullian wrote *Against Praxeas* and who Praxeas might have been.

As we proceed, we will dive into some deep theological ideas. This can be intimidating. Many Christians, for example, believe in the Trinity, but if you ask them to explain it, they may be at a loss for words. This is where years of teaching this material will (I hope) enable me to explain these ideas in a way that is easy to understand.

In *Against Praxeas*, Tertullian is attacking a theological idea known as Modalism. Modalism appeared as a theological view within Christianity in the second century and was condemned as heresy. (But the idea is still around in Christianity today.)

Here is the reasoning behind Modalism. How can we claim that there is only one God, but we speak of him as Father, Son, and Holy Spirit? Modalism says that Father, Son, and Holy Spirit are three modes—like three faces—of the same person. It is as if God is an actor on a stage with three different masks. When he created the world, he wore his "Father" mask; when he came to earth, he put on his "Son" mask; and when he leads believers to divine truth and performs works of power, he puts on his "Holy Spirit" mask.

Why did the church reject this idea? They did so because Modalism argues that the Father *is* the Son, and the Son *is* the Spirit, and the Spirit *is* the Father. But in Scripture Jesus clearly refers to the Father. He prays to the Father (e.g., Matt. 26:42; John 11:41–42; 17), and he cries out to the Father from the cross (Matt. 27:46; Mark 15:34; Luke 23:34, 46). If Jesus is the Father, then he is talking to himself in these instances. Jesus also says that he is going away and will ask the Father to send the Spirit (John 14:16), and that it is better for the disciples if he leaves so that the Spirit will come (16:7). But if Jesus is the Spirit, then in this instance, we would be asking himself to send himself and, in effect, not actually going anywhere. How could the Son pray and talk to the Father if he is the Father, and how could he send the Spirit if he is the Spirit?

No, the church said, Modalism is a wrong understanding of God because it contradicts Scripture. It also denies the uniqueness of the Father, the Son, and the Holy Spirit.

So who was Praxeas?

Here the story gets even more interesting. The name "Praxeas" may be a pseudonym (false name) for a particular person—namely, a bishop of Rome. We have evidence that some of the bishops of Rome supported Modalism, and we also know that Tertullian was not a friend of the Roman church. At one point he left Rome under difficult circumstances. Many think he was upset because a Roman bishop had condemned the Montanists, a group (as we have seen) that Tertullian held in high esteem and saw as perfectly orthodox in their doctrine. Tertullian especially seemed to appreciate their emphasis on the role of the Holy Spirit in the lives of believers.

Not only did Tertullian disagree with the condemnation of the Montanists by the Roman bishop, but he also thought that the Roman church had no right to interfere with churches in other regions. This may explain the name "Praxeas," which can be translated as "Busybody." Tertullian may be writing not only against someone he thought was a heretic but also against someone who, in his view, was interfering where he did not belong. Furthermore, we know that Tertullian did not get on well with a particular bishop, Callistus I (bishop of Rome from 218 to 222). Other details in the text point more specifically to Callistus being Praxeas. We cannot say this with certainty, because

Tertullian does not name the bishop directly. But there is strong circumstantial evidence that Tertullian had someone specific in mind.

Tertullian on the Trinity

In *Against Praxeas* Tertullian's primary concern is the doctrine of God. He argues not about matters of preference but about one of the core teachings of Christianity.

He sets out to explain the Trinity using Roman legal imagery, another indication that he may have been a lawyer. As we will see, he provides the explanation that church councils will eventually agree on, and yet they pay no attention to him and instead struggle to get there on their own.

The two key legal terms for Tertullian are *persona* and *substantia*. In Roman law a *persona* ("person") is a legal unit that can own property. A *persona* could be an individual or a modern corporation, a collective unit that could own something. We should avoid thinking that *persona* equals "person" in English, because not every person could be a *persona* under Roman law. For example, children, slaves, and in some cases women could not own property. They are people in the modern sense but not in the Roman legal sense.

The other key term Tertullian uses is *substantia*, which gives us the English word "substance." A *substantia* is something that can be owned, but it does not have to be a physical object. For example, my computer is a *substantia*. It is a piece of property that I own. If someone steals it, that is a violation of the law. But a *substantia* is also what I am typing into my computer as I write this book. My ideas are what we now call "intellectual property," and that is also a *substantia*. If someone plagiarizes my ideas, they have also stolen my property because I own my ideas. My ideas are not physical, but I can own them.

Furthermore, a *substantia* can be possessed by more than one *persona*. For example, if I get together with my sister and brother to buy a vacation home for our family (which probably will not happen unless this book becomes a major motion picture starring Brad Pitt), each of us is a separate *persona*, and together we own a *substantia* (the house). Or here is another example: if two people go into business together, each remains a separate *persona*, but they co-own a *substantia* (the business).

A *persona* can own something, and a *substantia* can be owned. More than one *persona* could be equal "owners" of a *substantia*. But how does this relate to the Trinity?

The Father is a *persona*. The Son is a *persona*. The Holy Spirit is also a *persona*. Divinity—the fact of being God—is a *substantia*. Just as my siblings

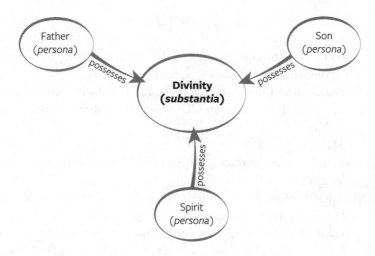

Figure 7.1 Tertullian's legal metaphor for the Trinity

and I could be three distinct but equal owners of a house, all three members of the Trinity are distinct, yet they all equally possess divinity. The three *personae* possess the same *substantia*. Three persons, one substance.

Praxeas, however, denies the status of *persona* to each member of the Trinity by collapsing them all into one *persona*. In the opening of *Against Praxeas* Tertullian goes on the offensive:

> He [Praxeas] claims that there is one only Lord, the almighty Creator of the world, so that out of this doctrine of unity he may create a heresy. He says that the Father himself came down into the virgin, that he was himself born of her, that he himself suffered, and that he himself was Jesus Christ. (*Prax.* 1)

Tertullian responds with a barrage of scriptural texts against Praxeas. He even claims that Satan himself knows that the Father and the Son are not the same but is thankful to Praxeas for spreading heresy. Tertullian rails against Praxeas for having done "a double service for the devil in Rome. He drove away prophecy and brought in heresy. He made the Paraclete [Holy Spirit] flee and crucified the Father" (*Prax.* 1). By condemning the Montanists, Praxeas drives out the Holy Spirit, and he replaces a correct understanding of God with the Modalist heresy.

Tertullian attempts to show that Praxeas's arguments are those of a "great fool." They are based on the distortion of only a few texts, while the Gospels show over and over the distinction between Father, Son, and Spirit. John's Gospel plays an especially important role, for here, most clearly, we see that the Father and the Son are one and yet still distinct. In the same passage Jesus says, "The Father knows me and I know the Father" (10:15) *and* "I and the Father are one" (10:30). The Spirit is also divine but is neither the Father nor the Son. In commenting on John's Gospel, Tertullian says, "The connection of the Father in the Son and of the Son in the Paraclete yields three connected persons who are still distinct from each other. These three are one, but not one" (*Prax.* 25).

The Father, the Son, and the Spirit are not one *persona*. That would be Modalism. So how are the three one? All three of them share a *substantia*, which is divinity. This is Roman legal language.

Tertullian, like the authors of Scripture, attempts to explain in human words divine mysteries that ultimately are beyond human words. He uses Roman legal language because that is most familiar to his audience.[1] A person does not have to be a lawyer to understand the basic concept of "owner" and "property," just as we understand those concepts today even if we are not attorneys.

To truly understand everything about God, we would have to be God. But as Paul writes, we see only "dimly" until we see God face-to-face (1 Cor. 13:12). Tertullian believes that Scripture argues against Modalism and in favor of the Trinity, so he attempts to describe the nature of God as best he can with the tools available to him.

Tertullian and the Early Church Councils

We can compare what Tertullian says with the creeds from the church councils. In the year 325 CE, the emperor Constantine calls a council at Nicaea, a city near the capital at Constantinople. The main topic of debate is the nature of the Son. Is he eternal, or is he created by the Father?

After more than a month of deliberation, the council issues a creed, or statement of faith ("creed" comes from the Latin word *credo*, "I believe"). We now refer to this as the Nicene Creed. The creed begins:

> We believe in one God, the Father almighty,
>   maker of all things visible and invisible.
> And in one Lord, Jesus Christ, the Son of God, begotten of the Father,
>   the only-begotten, that is, of the essence of the Father,
>   God from God, Light from Light, true God from true God,

---

1. Remember that among the Irish, Patrick famously used the example of the shamrock to explain the Trinity—one plant with three leaves.

> begotten, not made,
> of the same essence as the Father . . . [more follows about the life of
>   Christ].

The creed makes it clear that the Son was not made or created, and it also twice claims that the Son is of the *same essence* as the Father. There is no difference in essence or substance between the Father and the Son. Both share fully in divinity, just as Tertullian said.

In fact, when the creed was translated from Greek into Latin, the Son was described as *consubstantialis*. We see the word *substantia* in the middle of this longer adjective. But there is no evidence that the council read or paid any attention to the works of Tertullian. Unfortunately, over one hundred years after this African theologian offered his explanation of the nature of the Trinity in *Against Praxeas*—three persons, one essence—other parts of the church were still struggling with this basic truth. Thus Tertullian was over a century ahead of his time on this fundamental concept of God.

Tertullian's advanced thinking is not limited to the Son. His theology of the Holy Spirit is even farther ahead of his time. Tertullian says that the Spirit is also a *persona* who takes part in the *substantia* of divinity. Tertullian's strong doctrine on the Spirit may have influenced his support for the Montanists, who placed strong emphasis on the work of the Spirit. For Tertullian, the work of the Spirit is nothing to fear, for it is the work of God himself.

In *Against Praxeas* Tertullian states clearly, "The Spirit is God" (*Prax.* 26). From our perspective today, this is a standard part of the doctrine of the Trinity, but this was not always the case. Others were more hesitant and unclear about the essence of the Spirit. We see this if we return to the Nicene Creed of 325 CE. After the opening statement about the Father and a number of statements about the Son, the creed comes to the Spirit and says, "And [we believe] in the Holy Spirit." That is all the original creed says about the Spirit. It does *not* describe the Spirit as having "the same essence as the Father," as it does about the Son.

The fact is that in the period of the early councils some church leaders were not sure how to speak about the Holy Spirit. (Some argue that this is still true in some parts of Christianity today.)

In 381 CE, Emperor Theodosius I called another church council, this time in the capital city of Constantinople itself. Just a year prior, he had declared Christianity the official religion of the empire. But some ongoing debates surrounding the creed of 325 bothered him. So he called a council to sort things out for good (or so he thought).

The First Council of Constantinople issued an updated and clarified version of the creed. In churches today, Christians recite not the Nicene Creed of 325 but the updated Creed of Constantinople from 381. (Technically, scholars call it the Niceno-Constantinopolitan Creed.)

In the creed of 381 the section on the Spirit is more developed and states more about the role and source of the Spirit:

> And in the Holy Spirit, the Lord and Giver of Life,
>   who proceeds from the Father,[2]
>   who with the Father and the Son is worshiped and glorified,
>   who has spoken through the prophets.

The Spirit comes from the Father, is called the Lord, and is worshiped and glorified with the Father and the Son. However, the creed of 381 still does not say that the Spirit is of "the same essence as the Father."

When Christians recite this creed today, we assume that it means, or at least strongly implies, that the Spirit is also God. In that time, however, there was uncertainty about this. For a time, the chair of the 381 council was Gregory of Nazianzus. He was a theologian and bishop from Cappadocia (a region in the central part of modern Turkey) who eventually rose to become bishop in Constantinople. In the Eastern Orthodox Church he is considered one of the greatest thinkers in the history of Christianity and is often called simply Gregory the Theologian.

Gregory wanted the 381 creed to state explicitly that the Holy Spirit is God. Some resisted this point, while others attacked Gregory's leadership on technicalities of church law. In the end, Gregory decided that it was better for him to step down and let the council move forward than to fight for his position and be an obstacle to the council's progress.

When he announced his resignation in front of the council and the emperor, he took a final opportunity to restate some of his core ideas. Two of these were the unity of the Trinity and the full divinity of the Holy Spirit. In speaking of the Father, the Son, and the Spirit, he stated emphatically, "The three have one nature: God" (*Orat.* 42.15). All three are, without question, divine and should be worshiped as fully God.

He also did not miss the opportunity to attack Modalists, who were still around in his day. In the interest (they claim) of divine unity, they speak as if God wears three different masks. But actually, Gregory says, they destroy the Trinity.

---

2. The church in the West later added "and from the Son" to the Creed. This was a source of great controversy in the medieval church and was one of the factors in the East-West church split.

Gregory lost at the council but won in Christian history. He is often re-membered as a trailblazer concerning the theology of the Trinity and more specifically for the doctrine of the Holy Spirit. (Theologians call this "pneu-matology," from the Greek word for "spirit," *pneuma*.) But in fact, Gregory was simply walking on the same path as an African theologian from nearly two centuries earlier. Tertullian was the true trailblazer.

The Importance of Tertullian

We can only wonder how the history of Christianity and theology would have been different if the bishops at Nicaea and Constantinople had read and listened to Tertullian. How many third- and fourth-century heresies could have been avoided? How many fourth-century theological controversies would never have happened? If the church unified sooner in an understanding of the nature of God, how would history have been different?

We can only speculate about answers to these questions, but we can avoid the mistake that many Christians made in that time period. We can recognize the contribution of this theologian from the coast of Africa. We can appreci-ate his work and give his writings their proper place alongside those of other great thinkers of the early centuries of Christianity.

At times this chapter has been heavily theological. It is difficult to speak about God and the nature of God while staying only on the surface, for the truths of God are deep. But hopefully, we have come away with a greater understanding of Tertullian's importance for the doctrine of the Trinity (and perhaps we even understand the Trinity itself a little better). Tertullian used a metaphor from his world to try to explain the nature of God, and he argued strongly for the full divinity of all members of the Trinity.

For this, we should always remember him.

Part 3

Cyprian
of Carthage

8

The Life and Times
of Cyprian

┌─────────────────── *Key Ideas* ───────────────────┐

- The third century was a time of great challenge in the Roman
  Empire, and Christians were accused of being part of the problem.
- The emperor Decius responded to the crisis by attempting to
  enforce a return to traditional Roman religion.
- The emperor Valerian renewed and intensified Decius's policy of
  suppressing Christian practices, and this included the execution of
  bishops such as Cyprian.

Imagine a scenario with me. Imagine a context in which the economy is
bad. There is a recession and low confidence in the economic systems
and the leadership. Poverty is growing, and there is an increasing distance
between the upper class and the lower class. There have been troops fighting in
the Middle East for a long time. These wars have been an additional drain on
the economy and society. They seem to go on and on, and people are growing
weary. People are crossing the border. Some people are concerned about this
wave of arrivals, and some in leadership see it as an issue of security.

Here we see a battle between two different ideologies—two different ways
of thinking about society. Some argue, *We have a glorious past. We have been
the greatest power in the world, but we have lost our way. We need to get
back to those old values, the traditional values that made us great and will*

once again bring the divine blessing that we used to enjoy. Others respond, *No, we need to do new things. Things need to change. The old ways are done and should never come back. We need to put them behind us and move on.*

Disease has struck and made things even worse. People are dying by the thousands, and there seems to be no answer. And on top of all that, the weather patterns have been getting more extreme. Climate change has been detrimental to crops and put everyone, but especially farmers, under greater pressure.

Can you imagine it? When I present this scenario to students, they often think that I am talking about the contemporary United States. (And it does not matter what year I have taught this. Students have always found parallels.) When I have taught about this in other parts of the world, I have discovered that other places can also relate to many of these tensions.

But I am not describing the United States or any other place in the world today. So, is this just a hypothetical scenario?

No, welcome to the Roman Empire of the third century CE.[1]

The Crisis of the Third Century

This is the period that Roman historians refer to as the Crisis of the Third Century, the period from 235 to 284 CE.

— *Recession.* The empire has been struggling financially. A dynasty of emperors that ruled from 193 to 235 CE made devastating decisions. They wanted to grow the army, but they did not have the cash because the empire had not made any recent significant conquests. In the past, the army regularly conquered new territories and stripped them their wealth, which paid for future military campaigns. This process had nearly stopped, so this line of emperors devalued the currency. They began mixing cheaper metals like bronze and copper into the silver coinage so they could mint more coins. Inevitably, inflation soared out of control. The denarius had been the standard coin in the Roman Empire for three hundred years. It was a day's wage for the average day laborer. Do you remember when some religious leaders tried to trick Jesus with a question about taxes (Mark 12:13–17)? They brought him a denarius. But by the third century, prices were so far out of control that the denarius had next to no value, so it was taken out of circulation.

— *Wars.* On the empire's eastern border, the Sassanid Persians were pushing into Roman territory. By 235 they had already taken several major cities, and the Roman Empire lacked the military presence to push back.

---

1. This analogy is adapted from Mike Aquilina and James L. Papandrea, *Seven Revolutions: How Christianity Changed the World and Can Change It Again* (New York: Image, 2015), 11–14.

— *Immigration.* Rome lacked the resources to secure its northern border as well. Numerous tribes began streaming into the empire, especially from northern and central Europe. These "barbarians" included tribes such as the Goths, Visigoths, Ostrogoths, Vandals, and others, some of whom were being pushed westward by other tribes coming from central Asia.

— *Ideology.* Traditional values in that time meant worshiping the Roman gods. We discussed this in chapter 2 when we looked at why Christians were persecuted. Roman religion taught a give-and-take relationship with the gods: "I give so that you give." If humans worshiped the gods, the gods would allow the empire to flourish. People feared that this balance with the gods had been upset. When things went wrong, why did they go wrong? Most people believed it was because they had dishonored the gods.

Then along came revolutionaries saying, *No, we need to do things a different way.* Who were these troublemakers? Christians. Christians in the empire were saying, *The old ways are inferior. Those gods and goddesses are not real. It is foolish to believe in stone and wood as real gods. No, accept this new way, this better way of living.* In addition, Christians would not join the army because that would have required swearing an oath of allegiance to the emperor. In fact, some Christian sources state that members of the army were not eligible for baptism until they left military service. This further weakened the army.

For Christians, worshiping the one true God was the key to peace and divine blessing. For followers of traditional Roman religion, Christians were part of the problem.

— *Disease.* In 249 or 250 CE a plague broke out in Ethiopia. By the following year it had begun sweeping across large parts of the Roman Empire. It was highly contagious and at its height may have killed as many as five thousand people per day in Rome. Historians estimate that the plague claimed over half the total population in Alexandria, Egypt's largest city. The Roman emperors Hostilian and Claudius II Gothicus were among its victims, and it ravaged the empire for close to twenty years. The numerous deaths meant even fewer healthy men for the army. The exact cause has never been established, although Ebola has often been suggested.

— *Climate change.* A series of dry, scorching summers hit at this same time, further crippling a system of food production and distribution that already suffered from economic decline and the effects of the plague.

In the midst of all this uproar and turmoil, Cyprian became the bishop of Carthage in 249 CE. Can you imagine stepping into the job under these circumstances?

Decius and "That Old-Time Religion"

One other factor made Cyprian's context very challenging, and it relates to the traditional values mentioned above. According to Roman tradition, the city was founded in the year 753 BCE. This meant that 247 CE was the one-thousand-year anniversary of the founding of Rome. As the millennial anniversary approached, people became nostalgic. They began to think about the past glories of Rome. *Think about how powerful Rome was before these barbarians and Christians came along. Remember when we used to defeat the Persians? Tell the stories again about how we conquered here and drove out that group over there. Remember how great Rome was?*

Why had Rome been so great for nearly a thousand years? It must have been the traditional, old Roman ways, so enthusiasm for traditional values surged.

When I was young, I sometimes heard the expression "Give me that old-time religion." (It is also the title of a well-known nineteenth-century gospel song.) The expression refers to nostalgia for days gone by. *Back in the day, people loved God more, and we sang better songs. Everyone was more religious back then. Take me back to the good ol' days, when I used to go to church with my grandmother, and people dressed up for church. Give me that old-time religion.* Nostalgia has a way of distorting our perception of the

Figure 8.1 Roman emperor making an offering to the gods in honor of the three sacred animals: pig, sheep, and bull

"good ol' days," but it is still a powerful force. (I remember sitting in church in long, polyester pants and a dress shirt on humid, 95-degree days with no air-conditioning. Those "good ol' days" were not always so good.)

In the fall of 249 CE a new emperor rose to power. He was a capable general and administrator named Decius, and he was determined to restore the past glories of Rome. Part of this was bringing back "that old-time religion."

This required promoting the worship of the traditional gods throughout the empire and removing any internal threats from those who refused to worship. In December of 249 Decius issued an imperial decree. Everyone in the empire was required to go before their local officials and make a sacrifice in honor of the Roman gods. Each person would be given a receipt (called a *libellus*, or "little book") to prove that they had done this. Decius was trying to show himself to be an emperor in the model of the great leaders of the past, who were pious enough to please the gods.

Decius's logic was clear. *If we are going to get right with the gods again, if our economy is going to improve, if we are going to enjoy military victories, if we are going to restore the beautiful past of Rome, we all need to honor the gods. If you do not do this, you are identifying yourself as an enemy of Rome. You are in or you are out. There is no middle way.*

Decius was not setting out to be specifically anti-Christian. A person did not have to give up their faith to do this—in fact, for Decius *faith* was not really a factor. In Roman religion the emphasis was on what a person *did*, not what they believed. A person could believe in the God of Abraham and worship Christ, as long as they also performed a sacrifice in honor of the Roman gods. Failure to do this was seen as an act of treason against the empire and led to exile or imprisonment. Death was not a primary punishment at that time but sometimes resulted, especially after April 250, when torture was added to the penalties for those who refused to sacrifice.

It did not help Christians that the decree was issued at almost the same time as the arrival of the plague. Some blamed Christians. They said that the plague was the judgment of the gods because of these unbelievers. This fueled anti-Christian feeling across the empire.

The more prominent members of society attracted the most attention from the government, and this included Christian bishops. Fabian, the bishop of Rome, refused to sacrifice and was thrown into prison, where he died soon afterward. Mobs in cities such as Alexandria and Carthage turned on Christians as enemies of the empire and attacked. Dionysius, the bishop of Alexandria, narrowly escaped with his life and went into hiding in Libya.

Cyprian faced similar pressure in Carthage. He decided to flee to save his life, arguing that he needed to stay alive in order to lead his flock after the persecution ended. It was not a popular decision among everyone, particularly those who stayed and faced persecution. Without his leadership, many Christians in Carthage gave in to the pressure to sacrifice.

By the final months of 250, the persecution had started to lessen, but bishops such as Cyprian and Dionysius remained in hiding. Decius died in June 251 fighting the Goths on the northern frontier, and the Decian Persecution came to an end. Cyprian was able to return to Carthage.

By the time Cyprian returned to Carthage, the church there was being battered on all sides. The church was divided about what to do with Christians who had given in and sacrificed during the persecution. Cyprian also found his authority being challenged. From the outside, Christians were still being blamed for the plague. Much of the information about this plague survives in the writings of Cyprian, so it is often (and unfortunately) referred to as the Plague of Cyprian.

Meanwhile in the center of imperial power in Rome, disorder reigned for over two years. After the death of Decius three different emperors ruled within a two-year period. Hostilian died of the plague in late 251 and was replaced by Trebonianus Gallus, who was assassinated by his own troops in 253. Aemilian became emperor for a few months before he too was killed by his own soldiers, who put in his place a regional governor named Valerian.

Valerian and Intensifying Persecution

Valerian's name would become infamous on the pages of Christian history. Before the end of his seven-year reign (253–260 CE), he would renew Decius's policies to push traditional religion and even ramp up the persecution of Christians.

Christians avoided widespread harassment during the first few years of Valerian's reign. The emperor was busy fighting the Persians on the eastern front and the Goths on the front along the Black Sea. However, by 257 Valerian was turning his attention to internal matters as well. His views on the threats to the empire are seen by historians as remarkably similar to those of Decius, focusing on the worship of the traditional gods. Valerian's campaigns were not going well, so the gods must be angry. He decided that Christians had to be the reason, so he went farther than Decius by specifically targeting them.

In 257 CE he sent a letter from the Persian front back to the Senate in Rome with instructions for the suppression of Christianity. He focused on the Christian leadership and declared that all members of the clergy must perform sacrifices to the gods or face exile. Christians were also forbidden from having meetings—particularly in cemeteries in honor of the martyrs—because these were seen as "secretive." The Roman Empire had a long tradition of forbidding secret meetings because the government did not know what was happening at them. Valerian appealed to this legal precedent. As we saw in chapter 2, some of the rumors about Christians centered on what supposedly happened in the secret meetings of these "atheists."

According to one account of Cyprian's life, the bishop refused to sacrifice and was exiled that year to the city of Curubis (modern Kourba in Tunisia).

Valerian's 257 letter apparently did not bring results fast enough, so in 258 he sent another letter. It included a direct order to execute bishops and other Christian leaders. Christians from the aristocratic classes had to perform sacrifices to the gods, or they would lose their rank and be stripped of all their property. If they still refused to sacrifice, they were to be executed. There were by this time even Christians within the imperial household. If they refused to sacrifice, they would be forced into slavery.

Valerian hoped to kill Christianity by killing its leaders. Valerian was certainly not reading the writings of the prophet Zechariah, but he would have found the same principle there: "Strike the shepherd, and the sheep will be scattered" (Zech. 13:7, quoted by Jesus in Mark 14:27; Matt. 26:31). Once the leaders and the aristocrats were dead or had performed the sacrifice, the rest of the Christians would melt away. After all, there would be no one to lead their meetings or provide places for Christians to meet. Or so Valerian thought.

Sixtus II had been bishop of Rome for less than a year when he and seven of his deacons were targeted. Sixtus was arrested while leading a service in one of the Christian catacombs and was beheaded. His deacons soon followed him in death. The most famous of these was Lawrence. According to one tradition, after the death of Sixtus, Lawrence was told to hand over all the church's wealth. He asked for three days to gather it, and during that time he instead distributed all the church's property to the poor and needy of Rome. When he came before the governor three days later, he presented some of these underprivileged people as the true treasures of the church. He was immediately killed and is remembered as Saint Lawrence because he died as a martyr.[2]

By 258 Cyprian was back in Carthage, and the regional governor of Africa, Galerius Maximus, came looking for him. As in the year 250, the bishop had a choice to make: stay and die or flee and try to help the church in the future. Initially, he again chose to hide, but then he gave himself up.

2. In the Roman Catholic tradition, Lawrence is the third greatest saint of Rome after Peter and Paul. He is the patron saint of the poor, of deacons, of librarians, of comedians (because he tricked the governor), and of chefs—including specifically producers of barbecue. (This wins him points in my book.)

Galerius brought him in for trial and tried to convince the bishop to sacrifice, but Cyprian refused. The governor finally had no choice but to pronounce a sentence:

> For a long time you have lived an impious life, and you have gathered together a number of people as part of your illegal association. You have declared yourself openly to be an enemy of the gods and the religion of Rome. The pious, sacred, and honorable emperors . . . have tried in vain to bring you into line with our religious practices. Since you have been arrested as the head and ringleader in these terrible crimes, we are going to make an example of you for the others associated with you in these wicked practices. The authority of the law will be verified by the shedding of your blood. . . . It is decided that Thascius Cyprian will be punished by the sword. (*Acta Cypr.* 4)

Note the charges against Cyprian, which related directly to the restoration efforts of Valerian. Cyprian was charged with being "impious" and part of an "illegal association." He was accused of being "an enemy of the gods and the religion of Rome." Because he was the "ringleader" of this group, the Romans were going to make an "example" of him. Galerius thought that when the other Christians saw him shed Cyprian's blood, they would learn their lesson and fall into line.

On September 14, 258 CE, Cyprian died as a martyr by decapitation in the city of Carthage.

It turned out that Galerius was right, just not in the way he expected. Cyprian did become an example for other Christians. But instead of becoming afraid because of what had happened to their bishop, they became even bolder in their faith. The same thing happened among the earliest Christians when Paul was thrown into prison. See Phil. 1:12–14. For the centuries that followed, Cyprian was revered as the ideal African martyr. He stood for what it meant to stare death in the face without flinching.

Pontius was a deacon in Carthage at the time of Cyprian and knew the bishop well. In his *Life of Cyprian*, written very soon after Cyprian's martyrdom, Pontius reflected on Cyprian's death:

> Because he suffered in this way, Cyprian, who had been an example to all good men, also became the first example in North Africa who drenched [in blood] his priestly crown. He was the most important person after the apostles to serve as an example in this way. (*Vit. Cypr.* 19)

Killing the shepherd did not cause the sheep to scatter. Instead, it made his flock even more determined—although, as we will see, not necessarily united.

Few Christian leaders in history have faced as many challenges as Cyprian did. As bishop, he saw two rounds of imperial persecution and a plague. He paid for his faith with his life, and for that he is honored within Christianity to this day as the greatest of all the African martyrs.

But in his own time, Cyprian had to fight to keep his church, which endured so much suffering from the outside, from being torn apart from the inside.

9

Cyprian

On Forgiveness and Unity

─────────── **Key Ideas** ───────────

- Different Christian responses to persecution created a challenging situation, for those who had sacrificed to the gods and those who had refused were both in the church.
- Cyprian took a fairly rigorous position on the reintegration of the lapsed, while the confessors were more willing to offer letters of forgiveness.
- Cyprian faced challenges to his authority from those who saw him as too strict as well as those who accused him of being too lenient.

T
he persecution of the church that happened under Decius put Christians under tremendous pressure. In some cases, they had to decide between life and death, between keeping their property and losing it, or even between the demands of their faith and the demands of their families. It was a challenging time.

But even once the persecution ended, everyone could not simply go back to life as normal.

Different Responses to Persecution

As you recall from the preceding chapter, the emperor required every person to sacrifice and get a receipt showing they had done so. People in the upper class and Christian leaders were particularly targeted, but anyone could be asked to show proof of the sacrifice. Even a day laborer could be accused by a neighbor of treason for refusing to offer the sacrifice. Therefore, no one was really safe unless they had a *libellus* (receipt).

Not all Christians responded to the situation in the same way. We can group people in the churches into two broad categories. Both during and after the persecution, leaders had to deal with the fact that both categories of people were in the church together.

The first group are *the confessors*. These were people who refused to offer the sacrifice and therefore were thrown into prison, sent into exile, stripped of all their property, or some combination of these penalties. They *confessed* Christ at the moment of trial, and therefore lived up to Christ's standard in Matthew 10:32–33: "Whoever acknowledges me before others, I will also acknowledge before my Father in heaven. But whoever disowns me before others, I will disown before my Father in heaven." The confessors may not have been sent into the arena, but they still were revered because they had not backed down and had suffered as a result.

Within this category some did face execution. As numerous martyrdom accounts relate, throwing a person to the wild beasts was not a guarantee of death. Sometimes animals were not hungry or were otherwise not interested for some reason. We have accounts of animals having to be forced to attack people. Some people survived these attacks but bore on their bodies scars and other mutilations. Typically, we think of martyrs as those who died for their faith. But in the eyes of many Christians, surviving individuals had also given their lives, so they were in effect *living martyrs*.

Some, of course, did die. While these martyrs were no longer in the church, their example and sacrifice still mattered.

The second group are *the lapsed*. Not everyone believed that their faith was worth sacrificing their lives or their property for, so they simply offered the sacrifice. They *lapsed*, meaning that they were seen as having given up their faith. The term "apostate" (those who abandoned their faith) was also used to describe them. Surviving letters written by Cyprian, Cornelius of Rome, and Dionysius of Alexandria suggest that many Christians fell into this category. Perhaps they sacrificed out of fear, or perhaps they attempted to offer some theological justification. They might have said, *We all know from Paul's writings that these other gods and goddesses are not real gods, right? They are just wood and stone, so if I go and make an offering, I am not really making an offering to a pagan god or goddess. I am not really dishonoring God, because those are not real gods.*

As we have seen, Roman religion was not about belief or faith but about action, so Roman officials did not care if people believed in the gods or not.

People just needed to do the action. A Christian could therefore offer the sacrifice knowing that this was a useless action, and the government officials would not care. But in the eyes of some other Christians, such people abandoned the faith. They lapsed, and they were guilty of idolatry because they sacrificed to the pagan gods.

Within the overall category of the lapsed there was a distinct group, the "*libellus*-getters." Some Christians did not want to offer the sacrifice, but they also did not want to face the severe penalties for not doing so. They discovered a way around this situation. They needed a receipt, but there was more than one way to get one. Some appear to have bought them from other people. If a neighbor was not a Christian, a person could buy their *libellus*, and then that person could go back and get another one. The Christian was technically not offering the sacrifice, but they could show the necessary paperwork if it was demanded.

Others simply bribed their local officials. I understand that is difficult to imagine government officials taking bribes (insert sarcasm here), but in the ancient world sometimes this happened. Did these local officials actually care what Christians believed? No, not at all. We also know from numerous martyrdom accounts that the process of trying and executing people was sometimes more of a hassle than anything else. Therefore, Christians who had the financial means could sometimes purchase a *libellus*. Everyone was a winner, right? The Christian did not sacrifice and was protected, and the local official made some money on the side.

But in the eyes of other Christians, these people had failed to stand up for the faith.

Christian Unity?

We need to imagine the church in a city like Carthage, even while persecution under Decius was still going on. At any given meeting of the Christian community, all these categories of people might be present: confessors, living martyrs, lapsed, *libellus*-getters, and those who paid a bribe. What would that be like?

Imagine being in this situation. What if your brother died in the persecution? What if he was martyred in the most extreme sense? Or perhaps he did not die, but he is sitting next to you with extensive scars, perhaps even missing a limb. Or perhaps he is still in prison awaiting news of his fate. Across from you is one of the confessors. She refused to sacrifice and was thrown into prison. She may or may not have been beaten in prison, but she never denied her faith and was since released.

However, sitting behind you is a family that all offered the sacrifice to the pagan gods. When the decree was issued, they willingly went and committed idolatry. Near the front of the assembly sits one of the wealthiest men in the church. He owns significant property and is friendly with many local officials. He did not offer the sacrifice, but he bribed one of his friends in the government to give him a *libellus*.

So, think about the question again: What would that be like?

As the service continues, the time comes for the Eucharist, or Lord's Supper (also called Communion in some traditions). This was instituted by Jesus as an ongoing ritual that reminds the Christian community of its unity around the core of the faith. It binds all Christians together as a sign that everyone needs Christ and everyone is equal before Christ. You may remember that in 1 Corinthians 11, the apostle Paul is angry because the Lord's Supper had become a source of division, instead of unity.

How do you feel about the fact that when you go to receive Communion, you are shoulder to shoulder with people who gave in by sacrificing or working the system? The Eucharist involves sharing the bread and the cup to show unity, but do you feel unified with the lapsed? Do you feel joined in a bond of mutual love with someone who says, *Oh, I didn't really mean it. I just sacrificed to stay out of trouble*. Or, *I bribed someone to do it for me. But now I'm back and ready to worship Christ*.

As the bishop, Cyprian had to deal with this situation. It was a real issue, not a hypothetical one. What do you do with people who "gave up their faith," by either making the sacrifice or paying a bribe, and then come back and want to take the Eucharist with people who were imprisoned for their faith? How do you preserve unity? How do you

Figure 9.1 Mosaic image of Cyprian (Ravenna)

preserve community? And remember what Cyprian had done when persecution started. Taking the advice of other leaders, he had gone into hiding to preserve his own life until the pressure died down.

On the Lapsed

Cyprian was dealing with a delicate political situation. How could he honor the sacrifice of the martyrs and confessors while also caring for those who sought forgiveness? This was turning into a more complicated situation than the bishop could have imagined. It went beyond distinguishing categories of people in the church to the issue of church authority itself and even to the question of baptism (as we will see in chap. 10).

Carthage and Rome were in frequent conversation during this period, so what was happening in Rome must be part of our discussion. We should keep in mind that persecution was also happening in Rome, and Fabian, the bishop there, died within a few months of the beginning of Decius's persecution. Some Christians in Rome argued a rigorous position concerning the lapsed. They saw the sin of the lapsed as too serious to be easily forgiven. On the most extreme end of this position, some argued that the lapsed could never be restored to full communion in the church. This position was taken by one of the leading figures in the Roman church, a man named Novatian.

Because of the intensity of Decius's persecution, Rome did not have a bishop for nearly a year after the death of Fabian. During that interval a small group of influential priests, including Novatian, led the church. In a series of letters Novatian set out his argument against forgiving the lapsed. Idolatry, he argued, was a sin that could not be forgiven, at least not by the church. Those who surrendered their faith could never be fully restored into the Christian community, because only God could forgive that sin. A person could enter a period of penance, meaning that they were in a condition of begging for forgiveness for sin. Usually, after a length of time, a person could be restored to the church. But Novatian argued that penance for the lapsed had to last for the rest of their lives. Perhaps God would forgive them in the afterlife.

About a year after Fabian's death, Cornelius was elected bishop of Rome. He took a less rigorous position than Novatian. Forgiveness and readmission to the church would not be simple or quick, but it was still possible through the process of penance. Those who were truly sorry could ultimately be readmitted.

The Roman church was thrown into turmoil because a few priests wanted Novatian to be bishop, and the majority of Roman Christians supported him.

Cornelius disagreed with Novatian on the issue of forgiveness and saw him as a rival. Novatian was eventually kicked out of the church (excommunicated) and would go on to found his own church. (After that, Cornelius and others engaged in character assassination by making up all kinds of outrageous charges against him. Novatian was often accused of heresy, but his only "crime" was challenging Cornelius. Notably, Novatian wrote an important theological work defending the orthodox doctrine of the Trinity.)

The Roman church did not take the strictest position, and Cyprian was inclined to agree with their perspective. Carthage and Rome showed a common approach to the issue of the lapsed. But Cyprian faced a challenge to this position, and to his authority as a whole, from an unexpected and formidable source: the confessors.

Because of their courage and sacrifice, the confessors (including "living martyrs") were held in high regard in Christian communities. By this time, many believed that the martyrs had great spiritual authority and influence in heaven with God because they died for the faith. The confessors had been willing to give up their lives, so in the eyes of many they had charismatic authority and could apply it in this life and in the next.

This idea was not new. As we saw, in one of the visions in the *Passion of Perpetua and Felicity*, a bishop and presbyter begged Perpetua to settle their disagreement.

We might expect these confessors to be among the most rigorous when it came to forgiveness. After all, they had been willing to pay the ultimate price. However, ironically, the sources tell us that the confessors were more forgiving than bishops such as Cyprian and Cornelius. Some Christians went to the confessors to ask for forgiveness, and the confessors offered it to them: *We have the authority to forgive because we were willing to pay the ultimate sacrifice. And we are willing to forgive those who are truly sorry*. Confessors issued letters of forgiveness to the lapsed and promised to intercede with God on their behalf. These letters were soon being produced in large quantities and given out rather freely.

This situation caused two problems for Cyprian. First, the confessors were promoting a different policy from that of the bishop. Just as Novatian by his strictness threatened Cornelius in Rome, so the confessors threatened Cyprian because they were too lenient. Second, the confessors were directly challenging the authority of the bishop. According to church law, the bishop was the highest spiritual authority in his city or region. He controlled the practices of the church, including penance. The confessors were daring to speak and act in the place of the bishop, even directly against the bishop. They had in fact created an alternative spiritual hierarchy with themselves as the authorities.

Cyprian was trapped. He did not want to move to the lenient position on forgiveness, but he also could not be seen as criticizing or going against the confessors. This was a political minefield for him because while the confessors had stayed and faced persecution, he had gone into hiding. He was in a vulnerable position. Cyprian looked to Scripture for specific guidance on how to proceed, yet neither Jesus nor the apostles had faced a situation exactly like this. He would have to chart his own course.

Initially, Cyprian tried to walk a narrow line. He recognized the authority of the letters from the confessors, but he said that they applied only to a person on their deathbed. If a lapsed person wanted to be restored immediately to the church, the only way to do that was to go before the government officials and take back their sacrifice, thereby risking their lives and becoming confessors. Some accepted this compromise, including some of the confessors, while others claimed that the bishop had no right to question the authority of the confessors. If the confessors had issued forgiveness, then the person was forgiven—period. Cyprian was attempting to dance along a knife's edge and prevent open rebellion. Even among the other church leaders in Carthage, he was on the verge of being overthrown.

By the spring of 251, the persecution slowed even further, although Decius was still alive for a few more months. As Easter approached, Cyprian prepared to return to Carthage from hiding. At this time he wrote *On the Lapsed*, one of his most famous works.

He opened the work with an extended praise of the confessors and their courage. He skillfully wove this into his main argument: *splitting the church is a sin worse than idolatry*. The confessors suffered for the church, yet now some were in the process of ripping apart the very church that they had sacrificed to preserve. He wept because of "the hostile violence that ripped away a part of our own bowels and threw them away with cruel destruction." The confessors should mourn and suffer with their bishop, and Cyprian himself was pierced by the "cruel swords" of the rebels (*Laps.* 4). It was bad enough that the church was facing destruction from outside. Now it was also being torn apart from the inside.

Unity is the highest good, and unity must be maintained. Those who fight against unity destroy the church and have no part in it. He approached this issue first and foremost as a pastor. What will serve the church as a whole in real time and space? He could not deal with the issue as just a concept or a theological debate.

This work on unity may have helped some, yet it did not fully resolve the issue. In the late spring of 251, a group of African bishops finally met to discuss the situation. Being too strict or too lax could split the church. They compromised and divided the lapsed into those who had actually performed the sacrifice (the "sacrificers") and those who had gotten a *libellus* by buying it or bribery (the "certified"). The "sacrificers" would remain in penance until their deathbed. Only then could they be restored to the church and take the Eucharist. The "certified" could be restored immediately on a case-by-case basis.

Cyprian had the seemingly impossible task of trying to hold all this together and was under attack from all sides. He had to soften even his own position on forgiveness for the sake of unity, and he did it.

What Is the Church?

The debate over the lapsed could be interpreted different ways, but one of the core questions was this: *What is the church?* The way people thought about this question went a long way to determining their perspective in this debate.

I would like to offer two different images to help us understand the different perspectives in that time. To be clear, these images were not used in the third century, because they did not exist then. These are images from our time, but I believe that we can still use them to help us think about their concepts of the church. (These images might also allow us to reflect on our own concepts of the church.)

Is the church like a *clean room*, or is the church like a *hospital*?

Any company that manufactures electronic equipment or medical supplies has a *clean room*. This is a place built to be free of any contamination. For electronics and computer parts, there should be no dust, which could ruin the equipment. In a medical production facility, any germs or viruses would contaminate the products. In a clean room, workers wear masks, gloves, goggles, and full gowns. Everything has to be perfect, or at least as close to perfect as possible.

Should the church be like that? Should it be a place only for the clean, for the (seemingly) perfect? If so, then the lapsed should not be allowed back in because they would contaminate the church. Novatian represented this perspective, and to an extent so did Cyprian. They did not want to readmit the lapsed easily or at all, for this would make the church impure.

The staff in a *hospital* also wants to keep things as clean as possible, but their whole purpose is to welcome the sick and injured. They actually want the imperfect to come, for they have dedicated their lives to serving people in need. Doctors and nurses may confront people who end up in the hospital because they have made bad decisions, but they do not refuse to treat them.

Should the church be like that? Should it be a place where the goal is for people to get well by being there, such that the sinful and fallen would be the reason that the church exists? The lapsed and the *libellus*-getters had fallen, so the place they most needed to be was in the church, not kept out. They needed to be part of the community if they were going to get well. This was the more forgiving position taken by many of the confessors and some of the African leaders challenging Cyprian.

We may ask the same question about the church today. Is it a place for the well? Or are the doors open to the sick? Do we want to maintain a certain level of purity (or at least the appearance of purity)? Or should the church be a messy place full of fallen people? Or is it a mixture of both? Depending on how we answer that question, how do we respond when people fail?

This issue of the lapsed had broader implications and soon led to another debate, this one over the issue of baptism and rebaptism.

10

Cyprian
The Rebaptism Controversy

--- Key Ideas ---

- Both the rigorist and laxist parties opposed Cyprian and even elected their own rival bishops of Carthage.
- Cyprian argued that baptisms by both schismatics and heretics were not legitimate because those clergy were not pure. Therefore, people coming from those groups had to be rebaptized.
- Stephen I of Rome took a different position on the issue of rebaptism, and this led to a disagreement between the bishops of Carthage and Rome.

E ven after the death of Decius in 251 CE, Cyprian and the African church did not have peace and quiet. They were still in the midst of a plague, and rival bishops and their corresponding leadership structures defied Cyprian's authority.

Rival Bishops

On the one side sat the strictest group, "the rigorists." Apparently led by men sent to North Africa by Novatian and his followers, the rigorists argued that the lapsed could never be restored to the church. Only God could forgive the sin of idolatry, so the lapsed would die outside the peace of the church and face their eternal fate on their own.

In 252 the Novatianists ordained a Roman presbyter (elder) named Maximus as a bishop and sent him to Carthage to challenge Cyprian. The rigorists agreed with Cyprian that the bishop had the authority to control who was accepted into and back into the church. But they believed that Cyprian had disqualified himself as bishop by his lax standards. This strict party enjoyed wide support in some parts of Africa.

On the other side sat "the laxists"—many of whom were no doubt among the lapsed. Taking their cue from the more generous position of the confessors, they supported the immediate restoration to the church of all who asked for forgiveness. After the persecution ended, the confessors' political importance began to change. They were not quite as influential as they had been during the time of Decius, but the laxists did not want their openness to forgiveness to give way to the rigor of Cyprian or, even worse, to the Novatianists.

As early as spring 251, the laxist party had gained traction among a few African bishops. Their leader, Privatus, had been the bishop of Lambaesis, a city in the region of Numidia to the west of Carthage. He had been removed from office in 240 by a council on charges of heresy and misconduct, but now he was back and involved with church politics. He and a few other supporters ordained a man named Fortunatus, who had been a presbyter under Cyprian, to be the alternative bishop of Carthage. The lapsed of Africa had good reason to support this group, because they allowed the lapsed to return to their churches.

Thus, for a period of time there were three different people claiming to be the rightful bishop of Carthage.

Reunifying and the Question of Rebaptism

This situation lasted for several years, but eventually some sought to be reunified with other Christians. This led to another traumatic event during Cyprian's time: the rebaptism controversy.

In 254 or 255 a group of bishops from Numidia sent a letter to a gathering of the clergy (synod) in Carthage who were all in full communion with Cyprian. People from another group, certainly the laxists, wanted to rejoin the mainstream church, and they were uncertain what to do.

Technically, these people were *schismatics*, not *heretics*. Before we proceed, we should be clear on the distinction between these two categories. The word "schism" refers to a division or separation, so schismatics are those who are in some way separated from others in the church but still under the umbrella of the church. They share the same theological core, but they differ on some matter of belief or practice. As we saw in the preceding chapter, for Cyprian, schism was a very serious matter. In his eyes, breaking the unity of the church was worse than committing idolatry. The rival bishops of the laxists and the rigorists were technically schismatics. They could confess the same creeds, but they were still problematic.

Heretics, on the other hand, were separated from the church on some central theological beliefs. They did not just represent alternative Christian views on the issue or issues. They were seen as being non-Christian. They represented a break not *within* the church but *from* the church.

It appears that the Numidian bishops were asking what to do about schismatics, not heretics. Heretics were completely non-Christian, so all their rites and would-be sacraments were not recognized, including baptism. But what about schismatics? If a person was baptized in a schismatic group, did that count? Or should they be rebaptized in the dominant church (which Cyprian and his allies referred to as the catholic [universal] church)?[1]

An earlier church council in Africa stated clearly that any so-called baptisms by heretics did not count. But what about those wanting to move from the laxist church to the catholic church? It appears that people moving from the catholic church to the laxists were received without any problem, so should the mainstream church show the same acceptance? We learn from Cyprian's writings that Carthage had also begun to see the same thing happening. Some who had left Cyprian's church to join the laxists were beginning to return. What should be done with them? After all, they were not heretics in any technical sense.

Cyprian argued a rigorous position. There would be no distinction between baptism by schismatics and baptism by heretics. Neither one was legitimate.

Remember that Cyprian valued unity very highly, but he also valued *purity*. This is why he was slow to receive the lapsed back into communion with the church. In this case, it also led him to reject schismatic bishops as completely illegitimate. They were not inferior bishops; they were not bishops at all. In his mind, Christian unity was not at stake because these others were not true Christians.

---

1. The Greek word *katholikos* means "universal" or "international." I leave "catholic" here in lowercase to avoid confusion with the later claims of the Roman church to be the "Catholic" (capital C) church, meaning the only true church. As we will see in this chapter, Cyprian considered himself part of the catholic church, but he was not in agreement with the church in Rome on the issue of rebaptism.

Courtesy of Robin M. Jensen

Figure 10.1 Baptistery at Tipasa

In order for the African church to be unified and pure, the group of African bishops as a whole (the "college" of bishops) also had to be unified and pure. Cyprian did not believe that each individual bishop had separate and independent authority going back to the apostles. He believed that the college of bishops as a group had authority from the apostles as a group. Any schismatic or heretic among that group would contaminate the entire college.

The rigorous and laxist alternative bishops in Africa were false, and therefore their so-called sacraments were false. Baptism, the Eucharist, penance—any activity performed under the authority of a schismatic bishop—was void because these contaminated, counterfeit bishops did not have the spiritual authority to confer the Holy Spirit or offer forgiveness.

Cyprian was arguing for a strong sense of church authority focused on the bishops. This was consistent with his views on the lapsed. As you may recall from chapter 9, Cyprian was concerned because some confessors were offering forgiveness too easily and therefore undermining his authority as the bishop.

In Cyprian's eyes, he was arguing not for rebaptism but simply for baptism, because schismatics had no standing or spiritual power. Because they were impure, they could not perform the sacraments. In other words, baptism was effective only if performed by a "proper" bishop, and it was effective only *because* it was performed by a "proper" bishop. The grace of God in baptism had to flow through a pure conduit.

In Cyprian's writings on the matter he attacked the impurity of the schismatic bishops. In a letter to Cornelius of Rome, Cyprian referred to one schismatic group as "a faction of desperadoes" (*Ep.* 54.1). He called Fortunatus, the laxist rival bishop of Carthage, a "fake bishop put in place by a few incurable heretics" (*Ep.* 54.9). Privatus, the leader of the laxist party, was an "old heretic who had been condemned long ago for many serious crimes" (*Ep.* 54.10).

Their personal impurities disqualified them from being bishops and, therefore, from administering legitimate baptisms. Therefore, anyone coming from their groups to join the mainstream church had to go through a process of being accepted for baptism and then baptized. Cyprian openly attacked both these impure bishops *and* any bishops who had betrayed their duty by recognizing the baptisms performed in schismatic churches.

Conflict with Rome

In 254 CE Stephen I became bishop of Rome. He was still dealing with challenges in Rome from Novatian and his alternative church hierarchy, so he was quite familiar with the issues raised by schism.

The year 256 marked a turn in the rebaptism controversy and a beginning of open conflict between the African church and Rome. In the spring of that year, Cyprian sent several letters to Stephen concerning this controversy. He included a letter from the African bishops stating that they were requiring rebaptism.

Cyprian received a letter from Stephen that summer, and he must have been shocked by what he read. He described the contents of Stephen's response in a letter to another bishop, Pompeius, possibly the bishop of Sabrata in Roman Tripoli (modern Libya).

Stephen was irate that the African church was rebaptizing. In explaining his position, he distinguished between two parts of the baptismal process as it was practiced at that time across the entire Christian world, including Africa. First, a new convert was baptized, and immediately afterward the bishop would lay hands on them to confer the Holy Spirit. Stephen argued that only the second part had to be redone. Rebaptism was not necessary, even if the person was a heretic, not just a schismatic. Cyprian quoted from Stephen's letter:

> If anyone, therefore, comes to you from any kind of heresy, do not do anything that has not been handed down. I mean that hands should be laid on him for repentance, since the heretics themselves, in their own practice, do not baptize any who come to them from another group, but only admit them to communion. (*Ep.* 73.1)

The laying on of hands needed to be done by the bishop, but that was all. He claimed that this was the tradition that had been "handed down," so the Africans were wrong to depart from it. He then said that the mainstream/ catholic church should receive heretics without rebaptism, just as the heretics receive people from other groups without rebaptism.

Cyprian was furious. He rejected Stephen's right to tell the African church what to do—this was long before the establishment of the unchallenged authority of the Roman bishop (pope) in the West. Beyond that, he could not believe the content of Stephen's letter. He accused Stephen of trying "to maintain the cause of heretics against Christians, and against the church of God." By recognizing the baptism of heretics, he had "adopted the lies and the contamination of a foul washing" (*Ep.* 73.1–2). Cyprian was particularly disturbed that Stephen thought the church should follow the example of heretics: "The church of God and the spouse of Christ have become so evil that she follows the examples of heretics. For the purpose of celebrating the heavenly sacraments, [Stephen claims] the light should borrow practices from darkness, and Christians should do what the antichrists do" (*Ep.* 73.4). Note that any distinction between schismatics and heretics has disappeared. For Stephen to recognize the baptism of schismatics was just as bad as doing so for heretics.

The African bishop was unrelenting in his stinging assault on Stephen. The Roman bishop, he charged, had made himself dirty by forming an alliance with heretics and threatening the true church of God:

> Does he [Stephen] give glory to God, when he recognizes the baptism of Marcion? Does he give glory to God, when he judges that forgiveness of sins is granted among those who blaspheme against God? . . . Does he give glory to God, this one who has become a friend of heretics and an enemy to Christians, who thinks that the priests of God, who support the truth of Christ and the unity of the Church, are to be excommunicated? (*Ep.* 73.8)

Marcion was considered one of the most dangerous heretics of the second century. The Roman church had excommunicated Marcion because, among other things, he rejected anything Jewish. He taught that the world was created by a corrupt God of the Jews, not the heavenly God, and he rejected three of the four Gospels, leaving only parts of Luke. Cyprian was shocked that Stephen had now become a defender of heretics by recognizing the baptism of their followers. How could the Roman bishop claim to be glorifying God by supporting heretics? Even worse, Stephen had threatened to excommunicate Cyprian and the other African bishops, who "support the truth of Christ and the unity of the Church."

Cyprian returned to the concept of unity as he closed his argument against Stephen. To add force, he appealed to the words of the apostle Paul: "For it has been handed down to us that there is one God, and one Christ, and one hope, and one faith, and one Church, and one baptism practiced only in the one Church" (*Ep.* 73.11). This reference to Ephesians 4:5–6 supported Cyprian's claims that the one God has one church and that only that one church can administer baptism.

In the fall of 256, eighty-five African bishops gathered to consider the issue. They read the letters of Cyprian and Stephen and came to a unanimous decision. Those who had first been baptized by schismatics or heretics would have to be rebaptized in the catholic church if they were to be accepted.

The African bishops flatly rejected the position of the bishop of Rome. They were unphased by his threats of excommunication. Obviously, they did not believe he had the authority to enforce it. And even more, they believed he had sided with the schismatics and heretics.

The disagreement between Cyprian and Stephen stemmed from a fundamental difference in their understandings of baptism. For Cyprian, as we have noted, the bishop's purity was a requirement. True baptism could happen only through a true bishop. A tainted bishop yielded polluted sacraments, not the holy sacraments of the one holy church. As Cyprian asked, "How can one consecrate water who is himself unholy and does not have the Holy Spirit?" (*Ep.* 73.5).

We do not have a record of Stephen's complete arguments because we do not have his full letter to Cyprian from 256. We have only those tidbits preserved by Cyprian and in the writings of several other bishops who became involved in the affair, Dionysius of Alexandria and Firmilian of Caesarea (in Cappadocia, modern Turkey). Dionysius apparently tried to reconcile Stephen and Cyprian, while Firmilian sided with Cyprian and charged Stephen with having surrendered any claim to being the successor of the apostle Peter.

From what we can gather, Stephen appears to have made two arguments in favor of his more lenient position. First, he claimed that he was following the practice of the apostles in not requiring rebaptism. We do not know how he made this argument, and there is no scriptural example of the apostles recognizing baptism by schismatics or heretics. Whatever he said was unconvincing to Cyprian and Firmilian, and both bishops took him to task on this point.

Stephen's second argument was that the effectiveness of the sacrament lies in the practice itself through the example and commandment of Christ, not in the purity of the one performing the baptism. In other words, baptism is entirely the work of God, so the identity or purity of the person placing the convert under the water is not important. (Theologians have a technical name for this, *opus operatum*, which means that a ritual has value in and of itself, no matter who performs it.) Thus, it would appear that despite all the upheaval that Novatian had caused for the Roman church, Stephen still recognized Novatian's baptism as valid.

It may be helpful to return to our question from the end of the preceding chapter: What is the church? If the church is like a hospital, does the doctor need to be healthy in order for the patient to get better—for baptism to be effective? Cyprian would answer, *Yes, if the doctor is not well, the patient cannot get well.* Stephen would disagree, *No, even if the doctor is not well, they can still help a patient get well.*

Some church historians have gone to great lengths to smooth over the relationship between Stephen and Cyprian. They point out that in other letters, Cyprian tried to downplay any direct conflict with Stephen. There certainly is an air of respect, but their correspondence still shows the tension of the situation. Firmilian saw all the relevant letters from that time, including the letter from Stephen to Cyprian. He recorded, in a letter to Cyprian, that Stephen went so far as to call Cyprian "a false Christ and a false apostle, and a deceitful worker" (*Ep.* 74.26). This hardly seems like the language of minor disagreement.

As far as we can tell, and despite the best efforts of Dionysius of Alexandria, the conflict between Stephen and Cyprian was never resolved. In 257 persecution broke out under Valerian, and Stephen was beheaded in August of that year. His successor, Sixtus II, had more positive relations with his African colleague, although both Cyprian and Sixtus were fatal victims of persecution the following year.

Legacies of the Rebaptism Debate

On the issue of rebaptism, the final chapter was far from written. The issue would come up again during the Donatist Controversy (the subject of the next part of this book).

In a different form, this issue appeared during the Reformation. While Martin Luther and some other Reformers continued to practice infant baptism, other Protestants argued that baptism of an infant was not real baptism because baptism requires an expression of faith. Thus, when a Catholic or a Lutheran joined their group, they required such people to be rebaptized—or in their minds, baptized for the first time. This group was called the Anabaptists, which literally means the "Rebaptizers." Because they did not recognize the baptisms of others, they were hated by Catholics and other Protestants alike. Tens of thousands of them died through persecution at the hands of other Christians. Some fled to the New World for the sake of survival. They are the ancestors of the Amish and the Mennonites.

In the contemporary church, some denominations believe that baptism requires a confession of faith and immersion baptism, so infant baptism does not count as a true baptism. They may require believer's baptism to join their church, and this can be offensive, for example, to a person's family. *Are you saying that what we did for you when you were a child did not count?* Some groups go even further and recognize only baptisms performed in their own denominational churches. Some Christians discount other forms of baptism to the point of questioning the salvation of others.

What about the identity of the baptizer? In the Roman Catholic, Orthodox, and some Protestant traditions, only certain people are permitted to perform baptisms, and this is usually indicated by ordination. In other Protestant traditions, any believer can perform baptism because this is the work of God.

And does the baptizer have to be spiritually pure? Some argue that certain pastors, priests, or bishops may be disqualified for moral or theological reasons, so they cannot administer the sacraments of baptism and the Lord's Supper. Others disagree, and they probably also disagree on the reasons that would disqualify someone. Denominations have divided and continue to divide over this question.

These examples from the Reformation and the contemporary church are not exactly the same as what Cyprian faced in his time. The theological issues were different in the third century, but one element remains the same: questioning the baptism of another Christian group can lead to complicated and divisive interactions.

Cyprian did not live to see the restoration of the unity of the church. In fact, little did he know that many of his ideas would be used as ammunition in an even worse fracture of the African church about a half century after his death: the Donatist Controversy.

Part 4

The Donatist Controversy

11

The Life and Times of the Later Martyrs

Key Ideas

- The emperor Diocletian came to power during a period of peace for Christianity, but he eventually took a turn toward emphasizing traditional Roman religion.
- Under the influence of Galerius, Diocletian issued a series of increasingly aggressive orders against Christians, which launched the Great Persecution.
- Diocletian targeted Christian leaders and their holy books. Some clergy faced torture or death, while others traded their books for their lives.

This chapter will set up the historical situation of arguably the most important political, ecclesiastical, and social event in the early African church: the Donatist Controversy. In order to understand the complexities of this controversy, we need to look at the background.

We will begin by going back to Cyprian and discussing how he dealt with the lapsed. We saw that some thought the lapsed could come back immediately, some (including Cyprian) thought they could be restored only right before death, and some said they could not be restored to the church in this life. We raised the question "What is the church?" Is the church like a clean room? Or is the church like a hospital?

With the rebaptism controversy, we built upon that image and asked, "If the church is like a hospital, does the doctor have to be well in order to help others?" In the case of the African church, if the bishop was impure, then was everything that bishop did also impure? Could a schismatic or even heretical bishop administer a legitimate baptism? Stephen of Rome argued that baptism was the work of God, so the baptizer's purity was not central. Cyprian strongly disagreed and argued that an impure bishop (or cleric of any kind) could not celebrate true sacraments. Many in Africa agreed with Cyprian's more rigorous stance on this issue. Once a bishop had tainted himself, he was no longer fit to be a bishop, and none of his sacraments were legitimate.

All these questions, from a new angle, came back during the Donatist Controversy.

The Rise of Diocletian and Galerius

Following the end of the persecution by Valerian (he died in 260 CE in Persia), the church experienced several decades of relative peace. The radical push for traditional Roman values at the Christians' expense lost some momentum. In fact, by the late third century, we have evidence from the African church and other places that Christianity was expanding. Christians were increasing in number, and their presence was becoming more obvious. Specific buildings in some cities served as Christian gathering places. These places were identified as churches, and people knew they were churches. Christians were no longer limited to worshiping behind closed doors in private houses.

In 284 CE Diocletian became the emperor of the Roman Empire. Diocletian was a brilliant administrator. Within two years he figured out that the empire had grown too large for a single capital and a single leader, so in 286 he divided it into an eastern half, which he ruled, and a western half, which was ruled by a fierce military leader named Maximian.

In 293 he further divided the empire into four administrative regions with a leader attached to each (although he was still the ultimate authority). It was called the Tetrarchy—literally, "rule by four." It was not that Diocletian was humble or wanted to share power. Rather, he realized that his policies could be implemented more quickly and effectively if the population felt the weight of more local centers of government. Diocletian's junior partner in the eastern part of the empire was another strong—and, as it turned out, bloodthirsty—man who had risen through the ranks of the military. His name was Galerius, and when he married Diocletian's daughter, he became both lower emperor and son-in-law.

Diocletian was a traditional Roman emperor. Like Decius and Valerian, he wanted to go back to the old ways, to "that old-time religion." He hoped to restore the glory of Rome by restoring the old ways, and his co-rulers followed his lead. Many of the coins from this period feature images of the gods and goddesses, and an anonymous poem written in honor of Maximian stated:

> You have heaped the gods with altars and statues, temples and offerings, which you dedicated with your own name and your own image, whose sanctity is increased by the example you set of veneration for the gods. Surely, men will now understand what power resides in the gods, when you worship them so fervently.

Diocletian and his colleagues were leading a religious revival. The piety of the emperors set the example for the wider populace and showed "what power resides in the gods."

Of course, their example would work only if the empire turned around, if the emperors could deal with the economic difficulties of the empire. Within a few years, they began to do exactly that. The reign of Diocletian is identified by historians as the end of the Crisis of the Third Century.

Diocletian established his capital in Nicomedia, very close to where the next emperor, Constantine, would later establish his own capital of Constantinople. Nicomedia had a sizable Christian population by this time. We know this from a man named Lactantius, who worked in the imperial court of Diocletian. Diocletian brought him to Nicomedia to teach Latin rhetoric and language, but while there Lactantius converted to Christianity. (Later, he wrote one of the most important accounts of the conversion of Constantine.)

Lactantius was one of many Christians in the imperial court. This movement was therefore quite familiar to Diocletian, and according to one source, the emperor could even see the city's church building from the balcony of his palace. Initially, Diocletian did not see this as a direct threat, or perhaps he chose not to see it as a threat because he was acquainted with so many Christians.

All this changed in 299. In that year Diocletian and Galerius signed a peace treaty to end a war with their great rival on the eastern frontier, the Persians (technically, the Sassanid Empire). Following this, they performed sacrifices in honor of the Roman gods and sought their guidance on what the future would hold. In Roman tradition, the priests sacrificed animals and then read their entrails to discern the guidance of the gods, but these priests were unable to see anything. They claimed that they could not perform their functions because there were Christians in Diocletian's household.

We now see this for what it was—an excuse by these priests to attack their religious rivals—but Diocletian and Galerius believed it. Diocletian, probably spurred on by Galerius, ordered all members of his household to perform a sacrifice and then sent out an order that all members of the Roman army must also sacrifice. Those who refused would be removed from military service, which would mean the loss of social status and likely financial ruin.

As we noted in chapter 2, there were periods of time when those serving in the army were forbidden from being baptized. According to Hippolytus of Rome, soldiers could not be baptized because they had taken an oath of allegiance to the emperor. If they had sworn loyalty to the emperor, they could not be loyal first to God as their only king. Apparently, by the time of Diocletian, that was no longer the case, at least not everywhere.

In 301 Diocletian visited Egypt and had open conflicts with leaders of the Manichean religion. (We will learn more about the Manicheans in part 5, on Augustine.) Like Christians, Manicheans did not worship the traditional Roman gods and were seen as threats to the empire. Diocletian eventually ordered Manichean leaders to be burned alive, but by 302 he changed the punishment to execution for the lower classes and hard slave labor for Manichean

Figure 11.1 Person condemned to the wild beasts (Tripoli). Christians would have died in settings such as this.

aristocrats. The emperor was beginning to take aim at the enemies of traditional Roman religion. Christians were the next obvious target.

Diocletian planned to enforce exile as punishment for Christians, but Galerius pushed him further. A visit to the oracle of Apollo sealed the fate of the Christians. Apollo was unable to guide Diocletian because of the "impious ones," and Diocletian was finally convinced that eliminating Christians was the only option.

The Great Persecution

In February of 303 Diocletian burned the church in Nicomedia and any copies of Christian writings there, and he put all the church's wealth into his own treasury. On the next day, he sent out an order for the destruction of all Christian churches and books, and Christians were forbidden from meeting anywhere in the empire. Later that month, a fire broke out in the palace, and Galerius convinced Diocletian that it was set by Christians. There was no evidence of this, but Diocletian executed a number of Christians.

Diocletian's commands concerning Christians intensified and brought about the beginning of what is known as the Great Persecution. Diocletian and his colleagues, especially Galerius, were willing to deal with Christians violently if necessary, just as Decius and Valerian had done. But their superior administrative abilities and political structures allowed them to be more effective in their efforts.

This began a reign of terror unlike anything Christians had seen previously, both in its intensity and in its duration. The persecutions under Decius and Valerian lasted only a few years and tapered off after about a year. When those emperors died, the persecution died with them. But the Great Persecution lasted nearly a decade, well beyond Diocletian's reign. Diocletian retired in 305 due to illness, but his son-in-law, Galerius, carried on the torment of Christians until 311. (Officially, Christians were not safe until two later co-emperors, Constantine and Licinius, issued an edict of toleration in 313, traditionally known as the Edict of Milan.)

Christian martyrdom stories from this period are numerous. Some certainly were based on actual events, while others may have been later literary creations. Setting a martyr story in the time of Diocletian was, for Christians in later centuries, very believable. This is an indication of the trauma that Christians suffered during this period and remembered later.

The long list of martyrs named in later sources from the reign of Diocletian includes famous figures honored as saints within some Christian traditions (primarily Orthodox, Catholic, and Anglican): Agnes, who died at the age of twelve or thirteen after a few spurned would-be lovers turned her in for being a Christian; George, a military commander who was executed for refusing to sacrifice to the gods; and Sebastian, another member of the military who was killed for treason.

But Diocletian was not concerned primarily about individual Christians, at least not at first. He wanted to use a more efficient approach to deal with the Christian problem. As mentioned above, he had already targeted Christian buildings and Christian books. If Christians had no place to meet, then this could loosen the strength of the communities and their ties to one another. An organized group of Christians might be willing to resist imperial commands in a certain city. Would they do the same if they were isolated from one another? Would Christians be more committed to honoring their God or more worried about others turning them in to the authorities?

Diocletian also knew the importance of books for Christians. Their sacred texts were at the center of their faith. This was known by government officials long before Diocletian. For example, in the year 180 CE a group of Christians from a town in Africa called Scillium was brought before the governor in Carthage. They were threatened with death, unless they offered a sacrifice in honor of the emperor and the Roman gods. In the middle of the trial the governor noticed that the Christian leader, Speratus, brought a box with him. The governor asked, "What are the things in your box?" Speratus said, "Books and epistles of Paul, a just man" (*Acta mart. Scillit.* 12). Even facing their deaths, these Christians still carried some of their sacred texts with them. This shows the importance of Christian books, especially the Scriptures.

Diocletian took the same approach that Valerian had taken, focusing on Christian leaders first. According to the February edict, government officials were empowered to confront Christian clergy and demand their books and church property. According to Lactantius, who wrote a history of these events, Diocletian sent out the order against Christians with one hand and tried to hold off the violent desires of Galerius with the other. Diocletian "attempted to observe moderation by ordering the business to be carried out without bloodshed, while Galerius wanted to have everyone who refused to sacrifice burned alive" (*Mort.* 11).

Diocletian's first edict was intended to appease the gods by suppressing Christian practices, but all "without bloodshed." Not everyone observed this intention, however, and from the start some regions saw murderous actions against Christians. According to Lactantius and the church historian Eusebius of Caesarea, within a few months there were strikes against Christians in Nicomedia, Palestine, and Africa. The bishop of Nicomedia, Anthimus, was hunted down and beheaded. Only in the far western part of the empire were Christians largely left alone.

In some places Christians pushed back, so in the summer of 303 Diocletian issued a second edict ordering the arrest and imprisonment of all bishops and priests. According to Eusebius, so many church officials were arrested that murderers and grave robbers had to be released in order to make space in the prisons (*Hist. eccl.* 8.6.8).

The situation became unstable. By the fall of that year, Diocletian tried to pull back on the persecution of church leaders. Any who were willing to offer the sacrifice would be released from prison. Eusebius tells us that some did so willingly, but others refused. Some local officials were so tired of the Christian "problem" that they released clergy anyway and said they had sacrificed, even if they had not. Eusebius, in his *Martyrs of Palestine*, even recounts the story of one priest who was brought to an altar, where the guards overpowered him, grabbed his hand, and physically forced him to drop a pinch of incense into the fire. Then the man was told he had fulfilled his duty and was dismissed.

Diocletian's attempt to regain control by (in his mind) generosity did not work, so in January or February of 304 he went the other direction. His fourth edict within a year was the most oppressive and violent of all, no doubt to the delight of Galerius. In order to remove any uncertainty about enforcement of the order, everyone—including ordinary men, women, and children—was required to gather in a public space to perform a communal sacrifice. There was no place to hide, and the price of refusal was death.

As had been the case with the earlier edicts, enforcement was not carried out evenly across the empire. Christians living in Diocletian's and Galerius's territories suffered much, while Christians in the western part of the empire fared better overall, except, it would seem, those in Africa.

After Diocletian retired in 305, Galerius became the primary emperor in the east, and his junior colleague was a man named Maximinus. Like Galerius, Maximinus was eager to spill Christian blood, and in 306 and 309 he even issued his own edicts requiring sacrifice.

Diocletian set out to end the suffering of the empire and restore the past glory of Rome. With encouragement from Galerius, he attempted to eliminate threats to traditional religion. The Christians were high on his hit list. Diocletian intended and attempted to kill Christianity by getting rid of churches, books, and leaders. Some historians believe that he retired confident that he had achieved his goal. The church, at least in the East, had been weakened significantly. Even Eusebius recorded that a "multitude [of Christians] . . . paralyzed in their spirits by fear, were easily weakened right at the start" (*Hist. eccl.* 8.3.1).

But Diocletian, Galerius, and Maximinus were all wrong. The church did not die, even in the areas of the worst suffering. Instead, the blood of the martyrs only served to intensify the commitment among those who did not cave in. As Tertullian wrote, "The blood of the martyrs is the seed of the church" (*Apol.* 50).

to sacrifice

Back to the Books

To finish setting up the Donatist Controversy, we need to return to the policies concerning Christian books. An important part of the first edict was the seizing and burning of holy books. Not all Christian leaders responded in the same way, and this created major problems in Africa later.

Let us try to imagine the scene when Roman officials or soldiers set out to enforce Diocletian's first edict. A group of men arrive and knock on the door of the local bishop's house. The bishop knows why they are there. Their job is to demand the books and any church property (especially money or precious metal). The books will be burned; the property will be surrendered to the authorities. The desire, officially at least, is to avoid bloodshed.

Now we must remember that this order came at the end of nearly forty years of peaceful coexistence with Christians. Some of these local officials grew up with Christians as their friends and neighbors. Christian and non-Christian members of the aristocracy had socialized, and perhaps their families had intermarried. Bishops were important figures in some communities beyond the church, and they had other ties. In the city of Abthungi, south of Carthage, the bishop Felix was related to the local official in charge of executing the imperial order there.

From the perspective of the bishop, were the books worth putting his life in jeopardy? After all, Cyprian himself had chosen to flee Carthage in order to avoid death during the time of Decius. His life was too valuable to the church in Carthage. Was not the life of a bishop or a priest worth more to the church than a few books that could later be replaced?

Sources suggest that some handed over books, some refused, and some found ways to work around the order. This band of thugs at the door may not have been able to tell the Gospel of Matthew from a shopping list, for they may have not had a literate person among them. Could they have distinguished a copy of Paul's Letter to the Philippians from a letter written to their bishop by another bishop? Probably not. Therefore, some hid the Scriptures and handed over other books instead. Did the agents of the government necessarily care, as long as they could say they had done their job? Not necessarily, it seems.

Eventually, however, the persecution lessened and ended, and bishops' different responses to persecution created a problem. What should be done about bishops who had handed over books, even if they were not actually the Scriptures? Like the lapsed in Cyprian's time, they had buckled under pressure. Could they be restored? Or, as during the rebaptism controversy, were they now disqualified as clergy? Could they still administer the sacraments or—and this would become important later—ordain other clergy?

In this question about the handling of books lay the seeds of a debate that tore the African church apart.

12

Caecilianists versus Donatists

Rival Churches

┌─────────────────── *Key Ideas* ───────────────────┐

- Controversy arose in the African church over what to do about bishops who had handed over holy books during the Great Persecution.
- In 311 Caecilian was elected the new bishop of Cyprian, but many rejected his election, so a rival church hierarchy was established by a group called the Donatists.
- The Roman church and several Roman emperors sided with the followers of Caecilian and attempted to suppress the Donatist church, in some cases with violence.

As the persecution in North Africa was winding down in 311 CE, there was good news and bad news for the church. The good news was that Christians and their leaders were no longer at immediate risk of losing their lives (or so they thought). The bad news was that some had given in to the demands of the Roman officials, and this now had to be sorted out.

The Return of Old Questions

The Donatist Controversy focused especially on the bishops. As we noted in the preceding chapter, some responded to Diocletian's edicts by simply handing over Christian books to be destroyed by agents of the empire. They determined that their own lives were worth more than the books. Some handed over other books and pretended that they were the Scriptures, also in order to save their own lives. Others, however, paid the price for refusing to hand over anything.

A rigorous approach to the lapsed had been the African church's policy during Cyprian's time, and it appears that many among the laity (nonclergy) applied that same standard to the bishops after the Great Persecution.

The Latin verb *trado* means "to hand over" something, so the bishops accused of handing over books were called *traditores*—literally, "the ones who handed over." (This Latin word is the source of the English word "traitor.") In the eyes of many, they were as bad as the lapsed during the time of Decius and Valerian. Under pressure, they collapsed and did not stand firm, even those who handed over books that were not scriptural texts.

During the rebaptism controversy, Cyprian had declared that lapsed bishops were no longer legitimate bishops. They had forsaken their holy duties, so they could not administer sacraments or perform any other clerical duties. Many believed that this same condemnation should be applied to the *traditor* bishops. Because they were impure due to their betrayal of the faith, they should have no standing in the church.

One more dynamic must be included in our conversation because it later became a critical factor. Recall that in the middle of the third century, Cyprian disagreed with the Roman church on the question of rebaptism and rejected the right of the Roman bishop to interfere with affairs of another bishop's region. At the beginning of the fourth century, there was still no "pope" with the recognized authority to tell other bishops what to do. The Roman church was influential in the West but did not have unquestioned authority. Many Christians in Africa followed Cyprian in believing that the Roman church should mind its own business and that, in the case of the lapsed and rebaptism, it was simply wrong.

The rivalry between Africa and Rome was about to be rekindled, for the issue of handing over books was another situation in which perspectives on the lapsed and the purity of clergy led to disagreement with Rome. These were not new questions in Africa. They were *old and unsettled* questions that were revived in a new situation and bubbled to the surface in the year 311 CE.

The Eruption of the Controversy

Mensurius became bishop of Carthage in 303 and had the challenge of being bishop all the way up to 311—nearly the entirety of the Great Persecution. He was not universally loved because he opposed the right of confessors to "interfere" in church government, arguing that the authority belonged to the bishops alone. As a result, some accused him of being an enemy of the martyrs, and he was unpopular with much of the laity in the African church. The author of the *Acts of the Abitinian Martyrs* also accuses Mensurius of being a *traditor* (*Pass. Dat. Saturn.* 20), although the text provides no evidence for this charge. (It may have been just another way to attack his reputation.)

Mensurius died in 311, right around the time that persecution was coming to an end. One of his deacons, Caecilian, was nominated to take his place. According to church practice, the election should have waited until the arrival of bishops from Numidia, a less urban region to the west that had been more cautious about Roman connections and more rigorous about dealing with the lapsed. The leading bishop of Numidia—at that time Secundus—traditionally oversaw the proceedings. However, the supporters of Caecilian must have realized that their candidate would not enjoy support from Numidia, so they rushed to hold the election before Secundus arrived.

His election was immediately questioned by many in Africa. Not only had the process been irregular, but for some Caecilian was tainted by his association with Mensurius. Mensurius was like Cyprian in that he argued for the authority of the bishop, yet he was unlike Cyprian in that he dishonored the confessors and martyrs. In fact, as we saw in chapter 9, the opening of Cyprian's work *On the Lapsed* was an extended passage of praise of the martyrs and confessors. The opponents of Caecilian therefore argued that he was against not only the confessors and martyrs but also Cyprian himself.

Following a call for help from the opponents of Caecilian, the Numidian bishops organized themselves against Caecilian and his allies. Led by Secundus, a group of seventy bishops declared Caecilian illegitimate and elected a man named Majorinus in his place. There are indications that Majorinus was supported by the majority of the laity in Carthage.

The Numidian bishops did not technically have the authority to remove Caecilian, even though they thought the original election was improper, so they were prepared with an accusation that they hoped would require him to step down. In the preceding chapter we briefly met a bishop named Felix from the city of Abthungi, south of Carthage. We noted that a relative of his was the local imperial official in charge of seizing and burning the Christian books and churches in that city. This same Felix was also among those who

had ordained Caecilian as a priest long before he had become a deacon and
then bishop.

The opponents of Caecilian alleged that Felix had been a *traditor*, that he
had handed over holy books to his relative and to the agents of the empire.
Because he had done this, he was no longer a legitimate bishop and could
not perform any sacred duties, including ordination. Felix was not a true
bishop, so the ordination of Caecilian was not legitimate. Since Caecilian
was never properly ordained as a member of the clergy, he could not be the
bishop.

The anti-Caecilianist bishops were applying Cyprian's argument that illegitimate bishops could not perform holy duties. Cyprian said that schismatics
and heretics could not perform baptisms. (To use the hospital metaphor, sick
doctors *cannot* make patients well.) The Numidian bishops claimed that *traditores* were just as polluted, and their ordinations were just as false. Caecilian
served under and was now the successor of a *traditor* bishop and had been
ordained by another *traditor* bishop. He was tainted on two fronts. Caecilian's
supporters disputed these claims vigorously.

Was Felix in fact a *traditor*? Historians disagree on whether he actually
handed over books. One source suggested that he may have worked out a plan
with his relative to make it appear to the imperial government that he handed
over holy books without actually doing so. Such fine distinctions would not
have made a difference to the most rigorous Christians in Africa. And in any
event, all that really mattered in that time was that many people *believed* that
he had protected his own life instead of the holy books.

The official charge against Caecilian was that his ordination was invalid,
but there was more to the story. While he was still a deacon, Caecilian offended
an aristocratic woman in the church of Carthage named Lucilla. She wore
a relic of a martyr around her neck and used to kiss it just before receiving
the Eucharist. Caecilian rebuked her for this practice. She was offended by
Caecilian's actions and no doubt interpreted them as evidence that he, like
Mensurius, did not respect the martyrs. When Caecilian was elected bishop,
she was part of the group that opposed him.

But that was not the worst of it. An even more potentially damaging piece
of evidence came out suggesting that Caecilian was not just disrespectful
toward the martyrs but had actually persecuted them. The *Acts of the Abitinian Martyrs* (a text produced before Caecilian's election) claimed to recount
the events of 304 CE, when a group of Christians in Abitina, a village near
Carthage, was arrested for holding an illegal Christian gathering. Their case
was sent to Carthage, where they were imprisoned while awaiting a trial that
eventually led to their executions.

Roman prisons did not typically provide food and water for prisoners, so these Christians from Abitina (considered confessors by that point) relied on help from the outside. Then a seemingly unthinkable turn of events took place:

> When Mensurius, so-called bishop of Carthage, polluted by the recent hand-
> ing over of scripture, repented of the malice of his misdeeds and then began
> to reveal greater crimes, he who had had to beg and implore from the martyrs
> pardon for burning the books, raged against the martyrs with the same resolve
> with which he had handed over the divine laws, thus adding to his transgres-
> sions even more shameful acts. More ruthless than the tyrant, more bloody
> than the executioner, he chose Caecilian his deacon as a suitable minister of
> his misdeeds. He stationed him before the doors of the prison, armed with
> whips and lashes so he might turn away from the entrance and exit all those
> who brought food and drink to the martyrs in prison, further harming those
> already wronged by grave injustice. People who came to nourish the martyrs
> were struck down right and left by Caecilian. . . . To keep the pious from the
> embrace of the martyrs and to keep Christians from a duty of piety, Caecilian
> was more ruthless than the tyrant, more bloody than the executioner. (*Pass.*
> *Dat. Saturn.* 20)[1]

Mensurius was a *traditor* who had begged the confessors for their forgiveness. Apparently, they offered it. And how did he repay this mercy? Not only did he neglect another group of confessors; he actually sent someone to prevent aid from being given to them.

Some Christians were bringing food and water to the prisoners but were prevented from giving it to them. Who stopped them? Was it the Roman guards? No. It was none other than Caecilian himself, acting on behalf of the bishop. He physically beat off those trying to help the "martyrs in prison." His behavior prevented Christians from doing their pious duty to the confessors. Because of his treachery, Caecilian's actions were worse than those of the pagan persecutors. The *Acts of the Abitinian Martyrs* goes on to recount that the glorious martyrs died not by the sword or in the arena with the wild beasts but in prison by starvation—a horrific fate caused by Mensurius and Caecilian.

Historians disagree about whether these events actually took place. Some believe they did, while others claim the story was entirely made up to damage the reputation of Caecilian. In either case, it appears that many believed it be-cause the behavior of Mensurius and Caecilian had made the story plausible.

---

1. All translations of *Acts of the Abitinian Martyrs* come from Maureen A. Tilley, *Donatist Martyr Stories: The Church in Conflict in Roman North Africa*, Translated Texts for Historians 24 (Liverpool: Liverpool University Press, 1996), 25–50.

Rival Bishops, Rival Churches

Two different men were now claiming to be the legitimate bishop of Carthage, both of whom were elected under unusual circumstances. One had the support of the official hierarchy, while the other was the people's candidate and had the support of the Numidian bishops.

The Majorinus movement grew quickly and in 312 even sent a bishop to serve their supporters in Rome itself. Victor of Garba was his name, and without a doubt the official bishop of Rome at the time, Miltiades, did not take kindly to the presence of a rival. Ironically, Miltiades himself was of African origin, and now he was being challenged by someone from his own region.

In 313 Majorinus's supporters appealed their case to Emperor Constantine, who had risen to power only recently. This case was far above his level of theological expertise. His goal was simply to maintain peace in the empire, so he handed the issue over to a group of bishops led by Miltiades. The case was supposed to be decided by a group of three bishops from Gaul because the Majorinus party did not trust the Roman bishop. Miltiades, however, changed the plan and added fifteen Italian bishops of his own choosing.

While historical sources are a bit unclear on the precise date, it appears that Majorinus died some time during 313, perhaps after the appeal was sent but before the meeting in Rome. Therefore, the appeal in Rome was led by Donatus, who probably had just been elected to replace Majorinus as the new rival bishop of Carthage. He would prove to be a formidable foe for Caecilian. But on this occasion, he never even had a chance to present the case. The bishops decided in favor of Caecilian, and another appeal to the Council of Arles (in France) in 314 was also unsuccessful.

At this point we should pause and look at the names of the different groups involved in the controversy. Caecilian's supporters began calling their opponents "Donatists" after the name of the rival bishop, Donatus. They called themselves "Catholics," a term that comes from the Greek word *katholikos*, which means "general or universal." They used this title in order to claim that they were in communion with the wider church, as opposed to the Donatists, who had split from the wider church. Later historians from some Christian traditions have continued calling Caecilian a Catholic (with a capital C) as a way of expressing that he was in agreement with Rome and therefore "right" in this debate. This use by historians may tell us more about their own theological convictions and denominational preferences than it does about the historical reality of the early fourth century. But the Donatists also laid claim to the title "Catholics," saying that they were the legitimate church.

To speak from an objective, historical perspective, I will refer to the supporters of Caecilian (and his successors) as the Caecilianists and the supporters of Donatus (and his successors) as the Donatists.

By 316 Constantine decided that this schism, which threatened the unity of the empire, had to be resolved. He sent imperial troops to seize Donatist churches and suppress their worship. For the Caecilianists, this was an example of the emperor serving the church by defending the true bishop and fighting schism—or even heresy, as some saw it. For the Donatists, this was yet another example of imperial persecution of Christians. Constantine was acting just like Nero, Decius, and Valerian. The fact that the emperor was persecuting them was proof that they were the true church.

After five years, Constantine pulled back on his failed policies against the Donatists and "left them to the judgment of God" (*CPD* 31.54). But the damage was done. Donatists had died as martyrs by the order of Constantine, so they would not abandon their cause now. They had to keep the faith and honor only the "pure" bishops, not the descendants of the *traditores*, who were supported by the heavy hand of the empire.

The competing church hierarchies continued to grow. Historians believe that larger cities along the coast may have supported mainly Caecilianist bishops, while most of North Africa leaned toward the Donatists. And yet, even in some larger cities, competing bishops and even competing churches were very close to one another. In the fifth century, Augustine recorded that the Donatist church in Hippo Regius was so close to his own basilica that they could hear the Donatists singing. (In case this seems odd, it is worth noting that towns of any size in the United States often have multiple churches of the

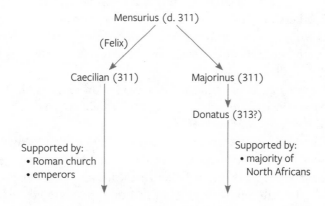

Figure 12.1 Caecilianist and Donatist bishops of Carthage

same denomination. Sometimes this is necessary due to the population, but often this reflects different theological camps within those denominations.)

A Century of Division

Both sides were firmly entrenched and unyielding, and the Donatists held their own church council in 336 CE. It was an impressive gathering of 270 bishops, and it addressed the issue of rebaptism of former members of Caecilianist churches. (Somewhat surprisingly, the Donatists decided not to require this.) In that same year, one of the leading civic officials in Rome, a man named Gregory, initiated some kind of violent action against Donatist supporters in that city. We know few details, but whatever happened caused Donatus to call Gregory a "stain upon the [Roman] Senate" (Optatus of Milevis, *Adv. Donat.* 3.3). Despite this additional opposition, the line of Donatist bishops at Rome continued.

About a decade later, in 347, the emperor Constans (one of Constantine's sons) made another attempt to heal the schism. He sent imperial ambassadors led by a certain Macarius, to bring the Donatists back into line. Bribery was apparently Constans's primary plan, yet the Donatists wanted no part of this. They did not trust any imperial agent by this time, and one of their rallying cries was "What does the emperor have to do with the church?"

The Donatist group that met with Macarius was led by a bishop named Marculus. After the meeting did not go well, the Donatist bishops were arrested and tortured. All were eventually released except Marculus, who was executed by being thrown off a cliff. According to a later anti-Donatist source, an extreme branch of the Donatists revolted and provoked Macarius and his troops. Whether or not this is how it started, there is no doubt that Macarius responded with a show of military force. His troops got out of control, and a slaughter of Donatists followed. For the Donatists, Constans was Valerian and Diocletian all over again.

Donatus was forced into exile and died in Gaul in 355. Still the Donatists persisted. Parmenian followed Donatus as the Donatist bishop of Carthage and served for nearly another forty years.

Only fragments of the writings of Donatus and his successors survive, and the story of the controversy has been dominated by the writings of two anti-Donatist writers, Optatus of Milevis in the fourth century and Augustine of Hippo in the fifth century. Optatus was a bishop in Numidia who wrote a long work against the Donatists. In it he presented the Donatists as schismatics and rebels from both the church and the rightful rule of the emperor.

He argued that the apostle Paul had told the Romans that Christians should honor all secular authorities, so the Donatists should have submitted to the emperors and their support for the Caecilianist bishops.

Augustine was less kind. He considered the Donatists to be heretics, utterly cut off from the church, and wrote a number of works condemning them. His hometown was in the middle of a region dominated by the Donatists, so he knew them well. But when he later became a bishop, he drew his authority from the Caecilianist line. He railed against the Donatists with great frequency and intensity. His perspective has impacted views of the Donatists down to this day. They are still widely spoken of as schismatics or even heretics, although few people today know who they were or what they were fighting to defend.

In 411 the emperor Honorius revisited the Donatist issue by calling a church council in Carthage. It was chaired by the Caecilianist bishop of Carthage, Marcellinus. Not surprisingly, the Donatists were again condemned, and this time they were declared outlaws. Their bishops were forced to surrender their churches, and the imperial forces ruthlessly suppressed Donatist worship. The persecution was so bad that even Augustine, enemy of the Donatists that he was, complained that Honorius had gone too far.

Courtesy of Robin M. Jensen

Figure 12.2 Donatist baptistery at Timgad

The Donatist Controversy was one of the most traumatic divisions of the early church. For over a century, the African church was split into rival church structures.

The question of the purity of bishops was still officially the heart of the issue, but as both sides struggled for the upper hand, another factor came into play. Both sides claimed that they could prove their legitimacy by the fact that they were in the line of the church's true martyrs.

13

Donatists versus Caecilianists

(Catholic) [handwritten annotation]

Church Split [handwritten annotation]

Rival Martyrs

Key Ideas

- Both Donatists and Caecilianists identified themselves as the true church because they were in the line of martyrs that went back to Cyprian and through him to the apostle Paul.
- The author of the *Acts of the Abitinian Martyrs* wrote the text in order to demonstrate that the Donatists were the true church.
- Optatus of Milevis and Augustine of Hippo were two of the primary voices arguing in favor of the Caecilianist church during the fourth and early fifth centuries.

In the preceding chapter we looked at the development of the Donatist Controversy in the creation of rival churches and leadership structures. The Caecilianists claimed to be the legitimate church because they were recognized by Rome and the emperor. The Donatists claimed to be the legitimate church because they had the "pure" bishops and probably the majority of the African Christian population. But neither side was able to convince the other by these arguments.

Both sides attempted to seal the argument in their favor by claiming that they were the true church because they were in the line of the martyrs going all the way back to the apostles.

Martyrs in North African Christianity

Christians in Africa suffered persecution at the hands of the Roman government in the second (Scillitan martyrs), third (Perpetua and Cyprian), and early fourth (Great Persecution) centuries. Here, as in many other parts of the empire, the veneration of the martyrs (scholars refer to this as the "cult of the martyrs") became an important aspect of Christian piety. The martyrs were significant figures because they had set the example by sacrificing their lives for their faith. As a result, in many places the words of Jesus became literally true—"If they persecuted me, they will persecute you also" (John 15:20)—and suffering was an expected part of being a follower of Christ.

The suffering church was the true church.

This way of thinking played a major role in the controversies that Cyprian faced concerning the lapsed and rebaptism. As we saw in the preceding chapter, the Donatists interpreted the military actions of Constantine and other Roman officials as proof of the fact that Donatists were the true Christians and had not surrendered to the empire. They saw themselves as the heirs to a tradition that went back to Cyprian, Perpetua, and even further—perhaps, most importantly, to the apostles themselves. They were the true church because they were the apostolic church.

Needless to say, the Caecilianists rejected this. They claimed to be the true apostolic church and accused the Donatists of being frauds.

In the Footsteps of the Apostle Paul

For both sides, Cyprian was a key figure in the debate over who was the true church of the martyrs. He was held in high regard by all African Christians because he had endured two rounds of imperial persecution and ultimately surrendered his life. But Cyprian's reputation as a martyr was enhanced by the fact that he was in a line of martyrs that went all the way back to the apostles, particularly Paul, who was revered throughout the Christian world as a model martyr.

We should take a few moments to summarize the traditions about Paul's death. The New Testament tells us that Paul came to Rome under arrest, probably in the early 60s CE, and stayed for two years (Acts 28). The Bible tells us nothing beyond that about Paul's fate. Some scholars think that Paul died at the end of that imprisonment, while others argue that Paul was released, went and preached more, and ended up back in a Roman prison later. Early Christian tradition was also divided on this point. In either case, the tradition says that Paul was sentenced to death by Emperor Nero. This is told first in the *Martyrdom of Paul* (the final section of the *Acts of Paul*), a text from the late second century that probably relies on much earlier traditions that were handed down by word of mouth.

According to several subsequent versions of the martyrdom, on the way to Paul's death, a pious woman gave him a cloth or a shroud to tie around his head so that he could cover his eyes at the moment of death. After he was decapitated, he supernaturally returned this bloody shroud to the woman, and it was able to perform miraculous healings. The Roman church claimed to have this shroud as late as the end of the sixth century. (Later traditions linked Paul's death to Peter's, but this was not part of the earliest accounts, which featured Paul as a model martyr in his own right.)

The story of Paul's death was crucial for the African church. In chapter 11 we saw that Paul's legacy played a role in the earliest surviving martyrdom story from North Africa, the *Acts of the Scillitan Martyrs*, which dates to around 180 CE. It is worth returning to this text now in more detail. This group of Christians was arrested in the village of Scillium and taken to Carthage for trial. In the middle of the trial, the governor noticed that they had brought something with them and questioned the Christian leader, Speratus, "What are the things in your box?" Speratus said, "Books and epistles of Paul, a just man" (*Acta mart. Scillit.* 12).

In the moment of facing certain death, the Christians were carrying and drawing strength from the example and letters of Paul.

We do not know which letters they had at the time, yet any number of Paul's letters could have been a source of encouragement. In Romans Paul writes, "The Spirit himself testifies with our spirit that we are God's children. Now if we are children, then we are heirs—heirs of God and co-heirs with Christ, if indeed we share in his sufferings in order that we may also share in his glory. I consider that our present sufferings are not worth comparing with the glory that will be revealed in us" (Rom. 8:16–18). In 2 Corinthians 11:24–27 Paul includes a long list of sufferings he endured for the gospel (being whipped, beaten, stoned, shipwrecked, etc.). Paul also writes to the Philippians of his joy even in the midst of suffering, for the gospel was continuing to advance in spite of, and even because of, his time in prison. They too should rejoice when they suffer (Phil. 1:12–30). These are only a few examples from Paul's letters and are almost certainly in the background of this text.

The *Acts of the Scillitan Martyrs* includes a specific allusion to another Pauline letter. When the governor heightens the pressure for the Christians to offer a sacrifice to honor the emperor and the Roman gods, Speratus replies, "I do not know the emperor of this age, but I serve instead that God whom no man sees nor is able to see with these eyes" (*Acta mart. Scillit.* 6). Speratus paraphrases a passage from 1 Timothy in which Paul describes God as dwelling "in unapproachable light, whom no one has seen or can see" (1 Tim. 6:16). At the moment of testing, Speratus and the others draw inspiration from Paul's words and actions.

Moments later, the martyrs learned that they would be following Paul's example in their manner of death. The governor declared, "Because they have obstinately persisted, although an opportunity was given to them to return to the custom of the Romans, it is decided that they will be punished by the sword" (*Acta mart. Scillit.* 14). They died by being decapitated with the sword, in exactly the same way Paul had died. In doing so, they were quite literally following in the apostle's footsteps, imitating him as he had urged several churches to do (1 Cor. 11:1; Phil. 3:17; 1 Thess. 1:6; 2 Thess. 3:9).

The accounts of the martyrdom of Cyprian also highlight the imitation of Paul. We have two accounts of this that were written soon after the bishop's death: the *Acts of Cyprian* (anonymous author) and the *Life of Cyprian*, written by Pontius, a deacon who served under Cyprian in Carthage.

The author of the *Acts of Cyprian* recorded several details that were meant to make the audience connect Cyprian's death with Paul's. After a short verbal exchange between the bishop and the Roman governor, the governor issued Cyprian's sentence: "It is decided that Thascius Cyprian will be punished by the sword" (*Acta Cypr.* 4). The Latin phrase used to describe Cyprian's sentence, "will be punished by the sword," is identical to the language used when the Scillitan martyrs were sentenced to death. Their deaths were connected to Paul's, and Cyprian's death was connected to theirs, so through them Cyprian was connected to Paul. Like the Scillitan martyrs, Cyprian was the ultimate illustration of following Paul's example.

As Cyprian approached his place of execution, "Many cloths and handkerchiefs were placed in front of him by the brothers" (*Acta Cypr.* 5). These details echo the stories about Paul receiving a shroud on the way to his death. Paul's cloth soaked up his blood and became a source of healing. The followers of Cyprian expected a similar thing to happen after the death of their bishop because he was dying in the same way as the apostle.

Pontius likewise highlighted the comparison between Paul and Cyprian in the *Life of Cyprian* (in a passage quoted at the end of chap. 8). After describing the bishop's death, the deacon tried to put this event into its wider context. He noted that Cyprian endured much suffering, just like the apostles did. By shedding his blood for the faith, he became the ultimate African example of endurance, second only to the apostles themselves: "Because he suffered in this way, Cyprian, who had been an example to all good men, also became the first example in North Africa who drenched [in blood] his priestly crown. He was the most important person after the apostles to serve as an example in this way" (*Vit. Cypr.* 19).

Cyprian was presented as the most important African martyr, not just because he was a bishop but, more importantly, because his death followed the model of the apostle Paul. Through his death, Cyprian became like an apostle for the African church.

Both the Donatists and the Caecilianists tried to claim this legacy of martyrdom for themselves.

True and False Martyrs: Donatist Voices

Who was the true church? Was it the church recognized by the emperor and the bishop of Rome, or was it the church of the "pure" bishops? The Donatists and the Caecilianists did not agree.

They did agree, however, on this point: the true church was the church of the true martyrs, the inheritors of the legacy that went through Cyprian and the Scillitan martyrs all the way back to the apostles. But which church hierarchy could rightly claim this?

Both sides staked their claim to being the church of the true martyrs through their attacks on each other. The overwhelming majority of surviving evidence about the Donatist Controversy comes from the Caecilianist perspective, but there is still enough material from the Donatist side to get a sense of their approach to the debate.

The Donatist perspective is shown well in the *Acts of the Abitinian Martyrs*, which we explored in the preceding chapter. This text contains the accusation that Caecilian, under order from Mensurius, beat away pious Christians who were trying to bring food and water to some confessors in prison.

The overall message of the text condemned the Caecilianists as a whole. In the opening of the *Acts of the Abitinian Martyrs*, the author made clear that the story would clarify who was and was not part of the true church:

> Once error has been condemned, let whoever rejoices in the Lord's truth read the records of the martyrs so as to hold fast to the Catholic Church and distinguish

the holy communion from the unholy. These [records] were inscribed in the indispensable archives of memory lest both the glory of the martyrs and the condemnation of the traitors [*traditores*] fade with the passing of the ages. (*Pass. Dat. Saturn.* 1)

The Donatist author claimed that his group, not the Caecilianists, was the legitimate church, for they were part of "the Catholic Church." The term "Catholic" was used to claim that they had remained part of the "holy communion." The Caecilianists, by contrast, were the schismatics—the ones who had left the church by following the "traitors" and had become part of the "unholy" communion.

The author wanted to make sure that the "condemnation of the traitors" was not forgotten in later times, and this was the reason for writing the *Acts of the Abitinian Martyrs*. These "records of the martyrs" would be lasting proof that some had departed from the church, while the true Donatist martyrs had "sealed with their own blood the verdict against the traitors and their associates, rejecting them from the communion of the Church" (*Pass. Dat. Saturn.* 2).

The importance of the apostle Paul for these Donatist martyrs appeared several times in the course of the story. According to the text, the Christian lector Emeritus was threatened if he did not hand over Scriptures. The governor asked him, "Do you have any scriptures in your home?" He responded, "I have them but they are in my heart" (*Pass. Dat. Saturn.* 12). The author highlights that this was an allusion to 2 Corinthians 3:3:

O martyr, mindful of the Apostle who had the Law of the Lord written "not in stone but by the Spirit of the living God, not on tablets of stone but in the tablets

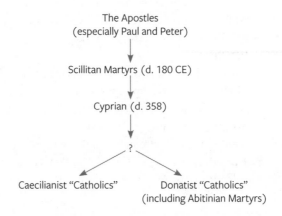

Figure 13.1 Caecilianist and Donatist martyrs: lines of succession

of the fleshy heart"! O martyr, most suitable and diligent custodian of the sacred Law! Trembling at the crime of the traitors, he placed the scriptures of the Lord within the recesses of his own heart lest he lose them. (*Pass. Dat. Saturn.* 12)

Paul served as the inspiration for Emeritus to place the Scriptures in his heart, where they could not be handed over, as the *traditores* had done. In the course of the story, two more of the martyrs also alluded to the same passage in 2 Corinthians by claiming that the Scriptures were in their hearts.

Paul's teaching and example run throughout the text, and the author returns to Paul's words in summarizing the overall message of the *Acts of the Abitinian Martyrs*, which is the separation between

> the church of the martyrs and the conventicle of traitors. . . . They are as contrary to each other as light is to darkness, life to death, a holy angel to the devil, Christ to the Antichrist. As Paul the Apostle said: "Open your hearts to me as children and do not be joined to unbelievers. For what sharing is there between justice and iniquity or what communion between light and darkness? What accord is there between Christ and Belial, what small share between a believer and an unbeliever, what agreement between the temple of God and idols?" (*Pass. Dat. Saturn.* 22)

Paul had warned the Corinthians to avoid communion with darkness, unbelievers, and the temple of idols (2 Cor. 6:14–16). The Caecilianists, who were led by the devil himself "under the pretext of most holy religion" (*Pass. Dat. Saturn.* 22), now embodied these dangers.

The author of the *Acts of the Abitinian Martyrs* left the reader with these instructions: "One must flee and curse the whole corrupt congregation of all the polluted people and all must seek the glorious lineage of the blessed martyrs, which is the one, holy, and true Church, from which the martyrs arise and whose divine mysteries the martyrs observe" (*Pass. Dat. Saturn.* 23). The Caecilianist churches were neither in the "lineage of the blessed martyrs" nor part of "the one, holy, and true Church, from which the martyrs arise." That honor belonged to the Donatists.

True and False Martyrs: The Caecilianist Response

In the middle of the fourth century, Optatus of Milevis became one of the primary Caecilianist voices against the Donatists. Both Caecilian and Donatus were dead, but the conflict between their successors continued, and the martyrs still played a key role.

Figure 13.2 Uppenna mosaic linking the Abitinian martyrs to the apostles. "Here are the names of the martyrs: Peter, Paul, Saturninus the presbyter. Likewise Saturninus, Bindemius, Saturninus, Donatus, Saturninus, Gududa, Paula, Clara, Lucilla, Kortun, Iader, Cecilius, Emilius, who died and were buried on November 8."

Optatus took aim at the Donatists both in Africa and in Rome. He saw the Roman context as an easy target because he could point to the martyr shrines of the apostles in Rome and who controlled them—that is, the Roman church, not the Donatists. Optatus argued that the illegitimacy of the Donatists was seen from the time of their first Roman bishop, Victor of Garba: "In Rome are the shrines of the two apostles [Peter and Paul]. Will you tell me whether he [Victor] has been able to approach them, or has offered sacrifice in those places, where, as is certain, are these shrines of the saints?" (*Adv. Donat.* 2.4.2). No, Victor could not offer sacrifice (the Eucharist / Lord's Supper) because he was not a true bishop and therefore did not have access to the martyr shrines of Paul and Peter.

Beyond this, Victor did not have a church in which he could lead worship. He was there "as a shepherd without a flock, as a bishop without a people. For neither a flock nor a people can those few people be called, who rushed between the more than forty basilicas in Rome, but did not have a place where they could gather" (*Adv. Donat.* 2.4.2). The fact that Victor did not have access to the martyr shrines or the churches showed that the Donatists were not authentic Christians. Caecilianists, who were in communion with the Roman church, were the true catholic and apostolic church.

In the early fifth century, Augustine of Hippo took up the Caecilianist case against the Donatists and similarly pointed to the apostolic martyrs as proof of which church was true. In his work *On Obedience*, Augustine tried to show that there was a line of true martyrs and a line of false martyrs:

> Precious in the sight of the Lord is the death of his just ones. Therefore the death of Peter is precious; therefore the death of Paul is precious; . . . therefore the death of Cyprian is precious. On what account are they precious? Because of a pure affection and a good conscience and a faith that is not false. That snake, however, sees this. That ancient serpent sees that the martyrs are honored and the temples are deserted. He carefully concocted cunning and poisonous plots against us, and because he was not able to wield influence over Christians by false gods, he created false martyrs. (*Oboed.* 16)

God rejoiced in the death of the saints, including the deaths of Cyprian and the apostles Peter and Paul, because they showed themselves to be true through their faith to the end.

The "ancient serpent," the devil, saw that the witness of these martyrs caused many to abandon the worship of the pagan gods, so he developed a more subtle plan. He attempted to lead astray the faithful by creating "false martyrs," a reference to the Donatist martyrs. Stories such as the *Acts of the Abitinian Martyrs* were not accounts of Christians facing persecution with courage. Instead, they were "cunning and poisonous plots" designed by the devil to deceive people into following the Donatist leaders.

In another sermon delivered on the annual feast day for the "birthdays" of Peter and Paul (June 29),[1] Augustine directly attacked the Donatists' right to claim the apostles as their own. While he rejoiced in the fact that the Caecilianists honored Paul and Peter, he claimed that the Donatists were on the outside looking in: "What will the heretics [the Donatists] say about these things? I think that even they celebrate the festival of the apostles. They

---

1. Ancient Christians describe the day of a martyr's death as that person's "birthday" because on that day they are born into heaven.

indeed strive to celebrate their day, but they do not dare to sing this song" (*Dies nat. Pet. Paul.* 9). The Donatists thought that they were also honoring the apostles. They even held a festival, but their efforts were useless, because they were heretics. They could not sing the song that belonged only to the members of the true church.

The True Church?

The Donatist Controversy was never formally settled, as far as we can tell from the sources. But the division between the Caecilianists and the Donatists soon became less of a focus when all Christians in Africa faced a more serious and common threat. The Vandals arrived on the shores of Africa in 430. They laid siege to Augustine's city of Hippo, and the bishop died during that siege. Less than a decade later, they pillaged Carthage itself.

In the time of Cyprian, the question was, *What is the church? A hospital or a clean room? And can an impure doctor (priest or bishop) heal you?*

By the time of the Donatist Controversy, the question had shifted: *Which one is the true church?* Those on both sides argued that walking into the wrong church with the wrong bishop was a theological death sentence. *We are the true church of God. They are a fraud of the devil.*

This conflict has haunted Christian history. On many occasions involving controversy between Christian groups, one side has used the term "Donatist" to condemn its adversaries. In the Middle Ages, reformers such as John Wycliffe (England), Jan Hus (Czech), Martin Luther (Germany), and Ulrich Zwingli (Switzerland) were called Donatists by their opponents.

In modern Christian settings, those accused of being too strict have been called Donatists. In Roman Catholicism, some have used the language to criticize the Society of Saint Pius X, which rejects many of the reforms made by the Second Vatican Council in the 1960s. In Protestant circles, particularly in divided or dividing denominations, those on the progressive side have used the term "Donatist" to condemn those who continue to argue for more traditional Christian approaches to issues such as human sexuality and doctrines such as the virgin birth and the physical resurrection of Christ.

Although it ended over fifteen hundred years ago, the Donatist Controversy remains relevant for the modern church, for it raises questions about the nature of the church and its leadership that are still being debated today.

Part 5

Augustine of Hippo

14

The Life and Times of Augustine

┌──────────────────────── *Key Ideas* ────────────────────────┐

- Augustine's Confessions recount his early life and his attempts to find satisfaction through physical pleasure, philosophy, and the Manichean religion.
- Augustine moved to Milan and came into contact with the bishop Ambrose, whose rhetorical skills inspired Augustine to listen to his sermons.
- After being baptized, Augustine wanted to withdraw into a monastery, but he was called into church service and eventually became the bishop of Hippo.

In this final section of the book we turn our attention to Augustine of Hippo. He was undoubtedly one of the most influential thinkers in the history of Christianity (particularly in the West), and in some church histories he is the only African to receive much attention. I sometimes attend conferences on early Christianity at which there are multiple sessions on Augustine in every time slot, and Augustine sessions are even double-booked because there are so many papers on him.

Augustine certainly was important, but I hope we can see by now that jumping straight to him while skipping over Perpetua, Tertullian, Cyprian, and the Donatist Controversy would be a mistake. Augustine was a product of his time and his context, and his work was deeply influenced by the African authors, leaders, and questions that came before him.

This chapter provides an overview of Augustine's life. Who was he? What events in his life journey set the course for him to become a powerful bishop and prolific author of sermons, letters, and theological works?

Much of what we know of Augustine's life comes from his autobiography: *Confessions*.

Young Augustine

Augustine was born in 354 CE in Thagaste (modern-day Souk Ahras in Algeria), a Roman trading town in North Africa. He came into the world at a time when Christianity was legal throughout the empire (it was not the official religion until 380), but the African church was deeply divided by the Donatist Controversy.

Augustine's father, Patricius, was not a Christian until near the end of his life. His dreams for his son were entirely secular. Augustine's mother, Monica, was a Christian. She did her best to raise her son in the faith, but it was not easy. As a young man, Augustine did many things that must have concerned her, but she kept praying and kept hoping. Eventually, her influence would impact her son and all of Christianity with it.

Augustine came to honor his mother as a saintly woman of God. The church agreed and later made her a saint. Eventually, a beautiful place on the beach was named for her: Santa Monica, California. One account claims that a Franciscan missionary, Juan Crespí, gave the city its name because he found two springs on the site that reminded him of the tears that Monica shed for her son during the wild days of his youth. The young Augustine was hard on his mother.

Monica wanted to influence him for Christianity, but his father was training him for public life. Augustine was intellectually gifted and came from a family that could afford to send him away to school, so at the age of twelve he was sent to a regional center of learning at Madauros. There he received a higher-quality education that helped him advance farther and faster in life. Madauros was not a big city, so a person who walks among its ruins today can be sure that Augustine walked those same streets.

Augustine then returned to Thagaste for a short time, but his boredom led him to pursue all kinds of pleasures. He famously recounted stealing a pear not because he wanted the pear but because stealing was wrong—and that made it all the sweeter to get away with. He stole just to feel the rush of stealing.

At last, Augustine's abilities and ambitions caused him to set his sights even higher. In 371, at the age of seventeen, he left Thagaste to study rhetoric in the big city, Carthage. It was the largest and wealthiest city in North Africa. Although he was officially going there for an education, he had other plans in mind as well. Augustine could not wait to see what the big city had to offer. (He was about the age of most college freshmen today, so some things do not change.)

By his own description in the *Confessions*, Augustine plunged headlong into the pleasures of the world—promiscuous sex, hanging out with a rough crowd, going to see lewd theatrical shows, and whatever else he could find to do.

But he was still doing well in his studies, and at this point Augustine knew deep down that something was wrong. He knew that he should be doing better, at least in terms of his intellectual life. While he continued his loose living, he also became more interested in philosophy. He was particularly attracted to Cicero, who believed that people could overcome their own weaknesses through self-discipline.

Two important things happened around this time. First, Augustine's father died, but not before he had received baptism. The man who had been pushing Augustine so hard toward secular pursuits had bowed the knee to Christ. Monica was thrilled; Augustine must have been perplexed.

Second, Augustine joined a group called the Manicheans. This was a religion that mixed elements of Christianity with other religions, especially another major religion of the ancient world called Zoroastrianism. We do not need to go into all the details of the Manichean religion, but here are the basics. Humans are stuck in a cosmic battle between light and dark, between good and evil. The good creates the human soul, while the evil creates the physical body. If a person can conquer their body through self-discipline, then they can defeat evil. But Manicheism also taught a version of fatalism, meaning much of this is out of your control. Many are in fact doomed to fail no matter how hard they try. Things are already decided. Augustine followed Manicheism for nine years, trying to find truth and comfort in this religion.

Augustine's recreational activities continued. During this period of life—at around age eighteen or nineteen—his live-in girlfriend gave birth to a son. Augustine eventually became frustrated with life in Carthage and went with his girlfriend and son to live in Rome and open a rhetorical school there.

The Challenge of Life Experiences

Augustine was pursuing his career aspirations in the capital city of Rome. He was following Manicheism and hoping that self-discipline could save him, although apparently he was not trying very hard. His mother continued to try to draw him toward Christianity. And although Augustine would later say it nicely, we have the impression that his mother was a bit of a nag at times. She was not letting this go.

Augustine finally returned to Africa, and his world was shaken when one of his closest friends died. In his *Confessions* he tells us about the conversations he had with this close friend in the days leading up to his death. His friend had been a Manichean along with Augustine but had converted to Christianity. Augustine tried to joke with him about his conversion, but his friend was not laughing. The fact that his friend took this so seriously began to shake Augustine's sense of confidence in how he was living.

When his friend died, Augustine could find no consolation anywhere. He wrote in his *Confessions*,

> My heart was completely darkened with sorrow, and everywhere I looked I saw death. My hometown was a torture chamber for me. . . . I asked my soul why it was so downcast and why this bothered me so deeply. But it did not know how to answer. . . . A strange feeling came over me, for now it was tiring to live and frightening to die. (*Conf.* 4.9)

His philosophical efforts and his pursuit of Manicheism offered no answers as he faced mortality. Yes, he had already lost his father, so he had felt the sting of death. But somehow it hit him much harder when death came to a close friend his own age. Augustine realized that if his friend could die, so could he. In my experience working with college and high school students, I often perceive among them a feeling of invulnerability until one of their peers dies. At that point they realize that life and death are serious matters. This is what happened to Augustine.

As he looked back on this experience, he alluded to Psalm 43:5: "Why, my soul, are you downcast? Why so disturbed within me?" At that time Augustine did not have the answer that the psalmist gives: "Put your hope in God, for I will yet praise him, my Savior and my God." Augustine was not sure where to put his hope. His soul did not have an answer for (to borrow a phrase from the Sherlock Holmes stories) the "Final Problem"—death itself.

Augustine reached such a level of desperation that he was totally overwhelmed. Living seemed too hard, but he was also afraid to die. He knew something was not right. He was shaken to the core and began moving away from Manicheism, which he had already been questioning seriously. He doubted that it could provide answers to the biggest questions.

The Turn in Milan

In 384 CE, not long before his thirtieth birthday, Augustine moved to Milan to pursue a position as a teacher of rhetoric. His mother followed him there, which probably did not make him happy. Now she could hound him from nearby.

In Milan God really ratcheted up the pressure on Augustine (even without his mother's help). The local bishop was a man named Ambrose, and it will help to understand a bit about his background. Ambrose was not a career churchman who had risen through the ranks as a priest or a monk. Instead, he had been a politician. His father had been the regional governor of Gaul (modern France), and the son was following in his father's footsteps. Ambrose studied law in Rome and caught the attention of certain government officials who then nominated him to be governor of a region in northern Italy. Milan was the capital, so Ambrose moved there in 370.

In 374 the bishop of Milan died, and there was a riot over who should be the next bishop. Ambrose was summoned to try to calm down the mob. As the people quieted down, someone shouted, "Ambrose for bishop!" The crowd erupted in support. Before he knew it, he was tapped to be the bishop. But Ambrose had not been baptized, so he was "fast-tracked" through prebaptismal training (catechesis) and baptism, then made bishop. He had been in the episcopal seat for about a decade by the time Augustine arrived in Milan.

Ambrose was a classically trained thinker and speaker, and for Augustine, hearing him speak was the best show in town. Augustine still did not agree with the content of Ambrose's sermons, because they were all very "Christian," yet he appreciated the bishop's skill as a public speaker. Ambrose was so brilliant and interesting that Augustine kept going back, although the messages bounced off his head and his heart—or so he thought.

Augustine was now hearing the message of Christianity from his mother on one side and Ambrose on another. But there was more. His worldview was also crumbling from the inside.

Augustine was still fighting to live his own way. He was still hoping that the pursuit of the pleasures of this life would bring him comfort and happiness. At this point in his life he prayed a famous prayer: "Give me purity and sexual restraint . . . but not yet" (*Conf.* 8.7). He wanted to continue his lifestyle for a little while longer, although at the same time the pursuit of physical pleasure was leaving him empty.

The intellectual life was his last stronghold, yet here too he was under attack from within himself. This brings us to my favorite passage in all of Augustine's writings. He recounted a day on which he and some of his intellectual friends were walking through the streets of Milan. He had been working on a speech in honor of the emperor, so he was feeling the pressure to put on a great performance. They passed a beggar by the road who was laughing and joking, apparently because he had drunk too much wine.

Augustine was struck by the irony of the situation. He had been laboring for years in order to achieve an important position in society, hoping that it would bring him happiness. And yet he was worn down by the anxiety that came with the position he had earned. This man, on the other hand, had found happiness thanks to a few coins he had been given, which he spent on wine.

Of course, Augustine realized that this beggar's happiness was brief, and his hunger and thirst would soon return: "Of course, his was not true happiness." Yet, the logical problem remained. If offered the choice between unhappiness and happiness, Augustine would choose happiness. But if offered the choice between his life and the life of this beggar, he would choose his own life. But he was not happy, and "my learning was no source of happiness to me" (*Conf.* 6.6).

Looking back later, Augustine would say that God was trying to get his attention through this experience as well. Augustine was running out of places to hide.

In summer 386, Augustine finally yielded to God. One afternoon he was in the back garden of a house, weeping in total despair at his inability to resolve his inner conflicts. Then he heard the voice of a child nearby singing a little tune over and over again: "Take it and read. Take it and read." He believed that God was telling him "to open [God's] book of scripture and read the first passage [he] saw." (Of course, this is not normally the best way to read the Bible. Scripture is not a Magic 8-Ball game.)

Augustine picked up a collection of the letters of Paul, opened it, and started reading. His eyes fell on Romans 13:13–14: "Let us behave decently, as in the daytime, not in carousing and drunkenness, not in sexual immorality and debauchery, not in dissension and jealousy. Rather, clothe yourselves with the Lord Jesus Christ, and do not think about how to gratify the desires of the flesh." It was like an arrow shot straight through his heart. Immediately, all his doubt went away, and he knew what he had to do. He had to set his sights and his hopes on God alone.

On this day, in this garden, the words of Scripture penetrated his hard heart in a way that had never happened before. In his *Confessions*, he later reflected on the years he had wasted running from God: "Too late have I loved you, O Beauty so ancient and so new. Too late have I loved you" (*Conf.* 10.27).

Augustine the Christian

Ambrose baptized Augustine in Milan on Easter 387 in a baptistery that you can still visit today. It is now called the Battistero Paleocristiano (Early Christian Baptistery) and was rediscovered in archaeological excavations beneath the Milan Cathedral, the second-largest Gothic cathedral in the world (see fig. 14.1).

After his baptism and conversion to Christianity, Augustine took Romans 13 seriously when it said to deny the flesh. (His son also died around this time, and we hear no more about the boy's mother.) But how could he escape the temptations of life? He decided to pursue life as a monk.

Augustine returned to Africa and founded a monastic community there. His idea was, it appears, to leave behind the society that he found so polluted with these impure thoughts and activities. He wanted to withdraw and be a monk, but he could not hide so easily. Time after time, Augustine kept being pulled into public life.

Eventually, and against his wishes, in 395 or 396 he was named the bishop of Hippo Regius, a city on the Mediterranean coast. Within about a decade, he went from being a hard-hearted, anti-Christian libertine to being a bishop.

He served as bishop of Hippo until his death in 430. The young Augustine had sought bigger and better opportunities, but the older Augustine put that behind him. Even if he had wanted to move, church law said that once

Figure 14.1 Baptistery of St. Thecla (Milan), site of Augustine's baptism by Ambrose

a person became the bishop in one city, he could not move to become bishop of another city. There was no "upward mobility" for bishops.

Much of Augustine's biography comes to us through *Confessions*. Most of the book looks back over his life, and he believed that God was at work even when he was unaware of it. The role of Monica, his training in rhetoric, the death of his friend—all these influences had been preparing him for what God had in store. Even secular historians and philosophers who ignore the theology recognize the importance of *Confessions* as the first major work of introspective autobiography.

At the opening of *Confessions*, Augustine makes one of his most-quoted statements: "You have made us for yourself, and our hearts find no peace until they find their rest in you" (*Conf.* 1.1).

Shadows of Augustine

Hippo is the modern city of Annaba, Algeria. On a prominent hill in the city stands a basilica named for Augustine and built at the end of the nineteenth century during the French colonial occupation of Algeria (see fig. 14.2). The statue of Augustine inside the church is believed to include a relic of one of his arms.

Marlena Whiting / Manar al-Athar

Figure 14.2 Basilica of Augustine (Hippo Regius). Rows of pillars separate the aisles in the central section of the church (nave), with the semicircular apse visible at the far end.

Augustine's church was actually in a valley below this modern basilica. We can still visit the remains of his Basilica of Peace. One account suggests that Augustine may have sat down when he preached, and the bishop's seat is preserved in the apse of the church.

When converts came to be baptized, he would have taken them to the baptistery just next to the church, which also partially survives (see fig. 14.3).

Figure 14.3 Baptistery of Augustine (Hippo Regius)

Photo by David L. Eastman

Next to the church is a residential building that archaeologists believe may have been the bishop's house.

In the next two chapters, we will look at Augustine's theology. As we do so, we need to keep in mind the experiences of his life discussed in this chapter. He chose to steal when he was young just for the joy of stealing, so he came to believe that children are not innocent. He tried to make himself better through philosophy and self-discipline, but he failed. In Manicheism he had to face the question of human choice versus fatalism. After his conversion to Christianity, he looked back on his life and concluded that God had been secretly working all along. All these experiences would later impact his theology, one way or another.

I should add one historical footnote to this overview of Augustine's life. When he returned to Africa after his baptism to found a monastery, he established rules for the monks. Centuries later, in 1244 CE, a group of religious hermits in Italy asked Pope Innocent IV to allow them to found a new religious order, and it was decided that they would follow the rules set up by Augustine. The Order of Saint Augustine (OSA) was founded and quickly spread beyond the boundaries of Italy. It still exists today.

Perhaps the most famous Augustinian monk in history was an intense young German who joined the Order of Saint Augustine in 1505. His name was Martin Luther.

15

Augustine

Theologian of the West

--- Key Ideas ---

- Augustine produced a large number of writings of different types, and his primary concern was almost always care for the church.
- He argued for the doctrine of original sin, which teaches that human beings are sinful at the moment of conception because they inherit guilt from Adam and Eve.
- Augustine also developed a relational model for understanding the Trinity and argued that the kingdom of God is not an earthly one.

Tertullian may have been the father of Latin theology, but Augustine was his more famous descendant (intellectually, not biologically). His surviving works top five million words. In this chapter we will consider the different kinds of texts he wrote and explore some of his most influential theological ideas. In the next chapter we will look at his theological dispute with Pelagius over questions of human and divine responsibility in salvation.

Different Reasons for Writing

Augustine never wrote in a vacuum. He was always responding to the needs and challenges of his time. His numerous works can be divided into a few broad categories:

1. *Works of theological reflection.* Augustine's *Confessions* fit into this category, for his primary theme is the work of God in his life even during his young, rebellious years. *On Christian Doctrine* is a guide to interpreting, teaching, and defending the Scriptures. Several other important works from this category will be discussed in this chapter. They include *The City of God, On the Trinity,* and *On Faith, Hope, and Love* (also known as the *Enchiridion,* or "Handbook").

2. *Commentaries on biblical books.* Augustine wrote several commentaries on Genesis, two of which offered metaphorical readings of the creation account, and another that offered what he called a "literal" account. (By "literal" he meant a reading that was historical yet also poetic and symbolic, because he believed that humans could never fully understand God's act of creation.) He wrote on Psalms, the Gospel of Matthew, the Gospel of John, Romans, Galatians, and 1 John, along with broader works answering questions about the Old Testament and the Gospels. These commentaries were meant to be useful for pastoral care and teaching.

3. *Polemical works.* Augustine spent a lot of time writing against people and groups that he considered heretics—always, in his mind, with an eye to defending the faith. You will recall that he was a Manichean for nine years, and he wrote six works specifically against them. Augustine rejected their cosmic dualism and tried to rescue other people who, in his mind, were still stuck in the error of Manicheism.

   As we saw in chapter 12, Augustine also wrote against the Donatists. He was taught and made bishop in the Caecilianist branch of the African church. He was pro-Roman and called himself part of the catholic (universal) church, while the Donatists were at best schismatics, more likely heretics. Their bishops were not legitimate in his mind, so in strong language he tried to convince the Donatists to come back to what he thought was the proper church.

   He wrote against many others in his desire to protect orthodoxy, including Pelagius, which will be the focus of chapter 16.

4. *Sermons.* Augustine was first and foremost a man of the church. His sermons reveal his theological ideas, but they also show the day-to-day realities of being a pastor and a bishop. In some of his sermons he deals with people from his congregation who were living unholy lives, and in other sermons he seems frustrated by poor attendance. (Modern pastors often find themselves dealing with the same issues.) Remember that the people in Hippo did not know they were listening to one of the most

famous figures in Christian history. He was simply their bishop, so some did not feel the need to listen to him all the time.

5. *Letters.* Some of these were written as polemical works, while others dealt with issues of church order or everyday affairs.

Taken together, these various kinds of writings give us a fuller picture of the career of a man who faced his share of struggles and understood the reality of caring for souls in the real world, not just in the lofty air of ideas and ideals.

And today he stands as one of the most influential people in the formation of Western theology. Roman Catholic theology owes him a great deal, and so do certain branches of Protestant theology.

Original Sin

Augustine argued for the doctrine of original sin. This a controversial topic because some Christians accept the idea and some reject it. And even among those who accept it there is disagreement about what it means for Christian practice. We are not going to dive into the deep end of those debates or try to solve them. The goal here is to give a summary of Augustine's views without trying to figure out who is right or wrong in the later interpretations.

We will begin with a general description of the doctrine. The doctrine of original sin teaches that sin is hereditary. Through the human process of reproduction, sin is passed down. Why? Because all humans are ultimately descendants of Adam and Eve (although for Augustine, Adam was the primary one to blame). The doctrine does not claim that all people are born *with a tendency toward sinning*; it claims that we are all in fact *sinners at the moment of conception.*

Figure 15.1 Mosaic image of Augustine (Palermo)

As far as we can tell, Augustine was the first to state the doctrine of original sin in this way. Those who support the doctrine argue that it is implied in Scripture, while those who oppose the doctrine say that Scripture shows that sin is not passed down from one generation to the next.

The key passage for Augustine is Romans 5:12. Here Paul is talking about the two Adams. The first Adam—Adam himself—brings sin into the world through his disobedience, while the second Adam—Christ—brings the antidote for sin. Here is what Paul says as translated from the Greek text: "Therefore, just as sin entered the world through one man, and death through sin, and in this way death came to all people, because all sinned."

Sin came into the world through Adam, and death followed. This applies to all people, "because all sinned." On the face of it, this seems to suggest that all people are under the penalty of sin and death because all have committed sins.

But Augustine was not reading the Greek text. He was reading a Latin translation, since as far as we can tell, Augustine did not read Greek. Where the Greek says "because," Paul uses an expression, *eph' hō*. It was a common expression meaning "because"—literally, "in that" or "due to the fact that." However, Augustine's Latin translation apparently said "in whom."

Therefore, as Augustine read the text, "death spread to all people *in whom* all sinned." Who is the person "in whom" all have sinned? It is the first Adam. Augustine argued that all people sinned "in Adam" because we are all his descendants. Adam's sin automatically becomes our sin and is passed down to all of us because we are all connected to him genetically.

In his work *On Faith, Hope, and Love*, Augustine states it this way: "It is said, and is probably correct, that infants are also guilty for the sins of their parents, not only the sins of the first humans, but also those of their birth parents" (*Enchir.* 46).

For Augustine, all humans inherit the sin of the first humans and their biological parents. We are all born with it. Supporters of the doctrine of original sin claim that Augustine makes clear what Paul implies in Romans, while opponents say that Augustine misunderstands Paul.

But how exactly is this sin passed down? For Augustine, it occurs through the sexual act because all sexual activity involves lust: "When it comes to the actual process of reproduction, the embrace that is lawful and honorable cannot happen without the passion of lust. . . . Whatever is born as a result of this burning lust is bound by original sin" (*Nupt.* 27). Augustine thought that sexual relations within marriage were not sinful as long as the goal of these relations was reproduction. However, lust was one of the results of Adam's sin, so wherever there was lust, original sin was present. (It may sound as if

Augustine was against marriage, but actually he was defending the value of marriage against some extremists who argued that true Christianity requires total sexual abstinence even within marriage.)

A baby right out of the womb is a sinner simply because the baby is a descendant of Adam and Eve. Babies are not born innocent. They are born with sin as, to borrow a modern phrase, a "preexisting condition."

For some Christians, this is the motivation for baptizing infants. They are born already out of relationship with God because of the sin of Adam and Eve. Augustine spoke about this in On Faith, Hope, and Love, where he referred to "the one sin that came into the world through one man and passed to all people, because of which even infants are baptized" (Enchir. 45).

Those who accept the idea of original sin also point to the Nicene Creed from 325 CE: "We believe in one baptism for the forgiveness of sins." This language is taken directly from Peter's sermon on the day of Pentecost (Acts 2:38). Here is the logic: if a baby is born a sinner, and if baptism is necessary to forgive sin, then a baby must be baptized in order to be forgiven. Not all Christians who baptize infants follow this exact line of reasoning, but some do.

The idea of original sin has been received differently across the history of Christianity. It became the official doctrine of the Roman Catholic Church and eventually gave rise to the doctrine of the immaculate conception, which was made official Catholic doctrine in 1854. Because Jesus had a human mother, he would have inherited sin through birth. However, this doctrine says that Mary was miraculously free from original sin, so sin was not passed on to him.

The idea of original sin was carried in a modified form into some branches of Protestantism, particularly those in the tradition of Martin Luther and John Calvin (Lutherans and Reformed/Calvinist Christians).

The Orthodox and some other Protestants reject the doctrine of original sin and argue that humans are born with a corrupted nature, but they are not sinners until they actually commit a sin. Yet even here there is division. Some still baptize infants to address the corruption of our human nature by sin (e.g., Orthodox, Methodists, Anglicans), while others do not baptize until children reach an age of accountability, when they recognize their sin and the need for forgiveness (e.g., Baptists, Christian Churches, Churches of Christ, Mennonites, Pentecostals).

Augustine's views on original sin became a major doctrine and source of debate in Christian theology, so no matter what our personal beliefs may be on the subject, it is worth noting the role that this African theologian played in its development.

The Relational Trinity

Augustine's theology of the Trinity is spread throughout his numerous works, but he deals with the topic most completely in *On the Trinity*. This massive work is composed of fifteen books written over the course of nearly thirty years in the later part of Augustine's life. In the introduction, he tells the reader a strange story. By the time he was in the middle of book 13, some readers became impatient and stole his copy of the work to publish it. Fortunately, he had other copies and used those to complete and publish the work quickly before the stolen copy had been distributed too widely.

He also tells the reader at the beginning that he is writing specifically against those who attempt to apply human reason and therefore misunderstand and misrepresent the Trinity. His concerns here remind us of Tertullian, who argued that philosophy and human reason could never lead to ultimate truth and could instead breed heresy. Augustine agreed. Some applied the limitations of physical bodies to a spiritual God, while others assumed that the divine spirit could be directly compared to the human spirit. Still others recognized that the topic was not understood through human reason but went on to speak about things they did not understand.

Augustine states that some truths about God do not fit within our normal thinking or understanding. Therefore, like Tertullian and others before him, he sometimes needed to speak about the Trinity using metaphors. At the outset, he summarizes the correct doctrine of the Trinity as it was stated in previous generations by those he believed were teaching the truth:

> The Father and Son and Holy Spirit share in one substance[1] and represent a divine unity. There are not three gods but one God. The Father has begotten the Son, and therefore the Father is not the Son. And the Son is begotten by the Father, and therefore the Son is not the Father. And the Holy Spirit is neither the Father nor the Son, but only the Spirit of the Father and the Son and also equal to the Father and the Son. (*Trin.* 1.4.7)

He reaffirms the basic teaching about the Trinity that Tertullian articulated. The Father, Son, and Spirit are one God and are all part of the unity that is God. They are also equal to one another. And he speaks directly against Modalism when he says that the Father, Son, and Spirit are also distinct from one another.

In *On the Trinity* Augustine uses various analogies and metaphors to speak of the Trinity. We will focus on one of his most famous and influential examples: the analogy of love. He recognizes that this is not a perfect analogy,

---

1. Augustine used the term *substantia*, echoing Tertullian.

yet it is helpful because "our feeble minds can perhaps understand this more easily through something that is familiar to us" (*Trin.* 9.2.2).

His analogy appeals to the human experience of love: "When I love anything, there are three things involved: myself, the thing that I love, and the love itself. I do not love love itself. No, I must love something, because there is no love unless something is being loved" (*Trin.* 9.2.2). Augustine tries to create a philosophical argument from human experience. We all understand, he says, that we cannot say we love unless we are loving someone or something. We are the lover, the love is something that comes from us, and the thing we love receives the love.

He applies this to the Trinity. The Father is the one who loves. The Son is the one who is loved ("This is my beloved Son"). The Spirit is the love itself.

Augustine certainly knew that the analogy was limited, but it has three important advantages. First, it addresses the question of how three divine persons can equally be God. We know from our own experience, he says, that love cannot happen in isolation. Love requires a sort of trinity: the lover, the love itself, and the object of the love. As Augustine says, "These three, therefore, are inseparable from another in an incredible way. Yet, each one of them is a substance [*substantia*], and all together they are one substance or essence" (*Trin.* 9.5.8). The lover cannot be separated from the love, and the love cannot be separated from the loved. There is a necessary relationship. All parts are equal and cannot be separated.

Second, this metaphor picks up on scriptural statements such as 1 John 4:7–8: "Dear friends, let us love one another, for love comes from God. Everyone who loves has been born of God and knows God. Whoever does not love does not know God, because God is love." God is the one who loves; love exists; we are the object of God's love. If we want to understand God, we need to

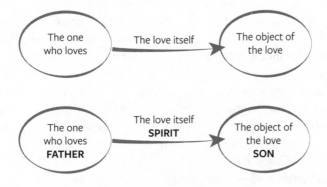

Figure 15.2 Augustine's relational model of the Trinity

understand love. Therefore, it is logical to apply our experience of love to our understanding of God.

Third, this metaphor emphasizes the relational element of God. God exists in relationship, not just with humans but also within God. Here Augustine is rejecting Modalism. At the beginning of *On the Trinity*, Augustine specifically condemns Modalism—the idea that God exists in isolation and simply changes masks to play different roles (see chap. 7, on Tertullian and the Trinity). No, Augustine says, God exists not in isolation but always in relationship. One God: Father, Son, and Holy Spirit.

Recognizing that his analogy ultimately falls short, Augustine states at the beginning of *On the Trinity* that human wisdom cannot help us understand some ultimate truths about God. However, by using the metaphor of love, Augustine wants to emphasize that God is essentially a relational being, and because we are created in God's image, we are also essentially relational beings. As 1 John indicates, the more we love one another, the more we reflect the nature of God. Or as Jesus puts it, "By this everyone will know that you are my disciples, if you love one another" (John 13:35).

God's Kingdom Is Heavenly, not Earthly

In August of 410 CE the city of Rome was sacked by the Visigoths, one of the so-called barbarian tribes that swept through Europe and swallowed up sections of the western part of the crumbling Roman Empire. For the first time in nearly eight hundred years, a foreign army had entered Rome.

This event was traumatic beyond belief. Christians in that period thought that God would protect their cities and, more to the point, that the saints would protect them. The tombs of Peter and Paul were in Rome, so certainly that city above all would never fall because the apostles would not let that happen. The idea that saints would protect their shrines and their cities was widespread in the ancient world (and continued into the Middle Ages).

But Rome fell and was ravaged for three days. Buildings were burned, and churches were looted (although the basilicas of Peter and Paul were left alone as sanctuaries). Some residents were killed or captured, abused, and sold into slavery. Others escaped the carnage and fled the city, and Africa was among the primary places of refuge. The church in Hippo would no doubt have welcomed demoralized and confused Christians from Rome.

Many were asking, *How could this happen?*

In the aftermath of 410, Augustine wrote his longest work, *The City of God*. In it he was fighting a war on two fronts. On the one hand, many non-

Christians said that Rome fell because of the Christians. Christianity had become the official religion of the empire only thirty years earlier, in 380. Some said that the traditional Roman gods were angry for being ignored and had punished Rome by sending the Visigoths. This was "that old-time religion" from the time of Decian, Valerian, and Diocletian. Augustine dismisses such thinking and argues instead that God spared Rome longer from the barbarians because the Christians were in the city.

On the other hand, many Christians wondered how God and the saints could let Rome fall. Augustine responds not by offering comfort but by challenging their assumptions. The problem is not that Rome fell. The problem is that they have misunderstood the nature of the kingdom of God.

Many thought that Rome was God's city, as if Christ and the apostles had established a kingdom on earth. Many thought that the apostles' tombs guaranteed the glory of Rome, but they were misguided. The true city of God is a heavenly city. Augustine tells his readers,

> Two cities have been formed by two loves. The earthly city is formed by the love of self, even disregard for God. The heavenly city is formed by the love of God, even disregard for the self. The former glories in itself; the latter glorifies the Lord. (*Civ.* 14.28)

Putting confidence in earthly power was not something neutral but actually showed disrespect for God because the earthly city and its leaders were corrupt and sought glory for themselves, not for God. With no hesitation, Augustine brings a stinging critique against anyone who puts their hope in an earthly power in place of the eternal city of God.

What Christ promised his disciples is what God promises us: citizenship in a heavenly city, the true city of God. Paul (Phil. 3:20) and Peter (1 Pet. 2:11) themselves understood this (see also Heb. 13:14).

History would show that many did not heed Augustine's words. In the Middle Ages many parts of Europe attempted to marry an earthly kingdom with a heavenly one. Religious leaders controlled empires and led armies into battle. Some sought to create their own city of God, but all those efforts would eventually fail.

Even today some may struggle to hear the message of Augustine. Some may believe that God favors one country over another or perhaps that their country will be stronger if Christians (at least those who share their political views) are in power. They may believe it is possible to build the city of God on earth.

Augustine would disagree.

16

Augustine

Debate with Pelagius on Grace and the Will

Key Ideas

- The idea of asceticism inspired Pelagius to teach that God gives humans the ability to do good but that it is up to humans to follow through.
- Augustine argued that Pelagius's views gave too much responsibility and credit to human free will and undermined the grace of God.
- Augustine's ideas included the notion of predestination and set up theological debates on grace and free will that have continued throughout the history of Christianity.

This chapter will explore Augustine's most famous theological dispute— a dispute with a man named Pelagius. The debate focuses on the state of humanity and the role and availability of God's grace for salvation.

The Roots of Self-Discipline

The roots of this debate lie in a wider controversy in early Christianity concerning the importance and limits of self-discipline. Some in the early church argued from 1 Corinthians 7 that the highest form of Christian life required extreme denial of the self. This led to the practice of "asceticism," a word that comes from the Greek term for "discipline" (askēsis). Ascetics (the people who practiced asceticism) denied themselves physical pleasures, including any food they might actually enjoy and sexual relations even within marriage. Ascetics believed that their discipline made them more acceptable in God's eyes.

One of the most famous examples of this lifestyle in Western Christianity was Jerome, a prominent Bible scholar and theologian who lived at the same time as Augustine. Jerome was from northern Italy and made a name for himself across the Mediterranean. He is probably best known for translating the Bible into the Latin translation known as the Vulgate. Jerome's translation stood out because he used the original Hebrew text for the Old Testament and the Greek for the New Testament. Before that, others had used the Greek translation of the Old Testament, not the Hebrew itself.

Jerome was one of the most educated and revered men of his time, and he modeled an ascetic life. His example influenced many others, and many in and around Rome admired him.

Around 380 CE, Pelagius moved to Rome. Augustine (Ep. 186.1) and Jerome (Comm. Jer. bk. 1, prol.; bk. 3, prol.) agree that he originally came from Britain (Jerome accuses him of being "stuffed full of Scottish porridge"). Like Jerome, he was well educated. Pelagius and others were inspired by the rigorous self-discipline of Jerome and other ascetics, but when they looked at society around them, they saw spiritual and moral laziness. Sin was running rampant because Christians were not disciplining themselves.

Pelagius concluded that Christians were acting in unholy ways because they chose to act that way. They chose to be morally loose. They chose to sin over and over again and break their relationship with God. God had given them the Scriptures and other tools to live a holy life, but they were not using them. But if humans could choose to sin, then they could also choose not to sin. Pelagius began to teach a strict form of self-denial and moralism. It is possible to be pleasing in God's eyes. We just need to discipline ourselves to do it. Although he had been inspired by Jerome, Pelagius had now gone off on his own. This new teaching did not reflect what Jerome taught. In fact, Jerome and Pelagius later had an open conflict in Jerusalem over Pelagius's ideas.

Augustine Gets Involved

In around 410, perhaps just before the sack of Rome by the Visigoths, Pelagius and some of his supporters left Rome for Africa. There he came into direct conflict with Augustine.

Augustine saw the teachings of Pelagius as incorrect and dangerous. Teaching people that they could earn God's favor by self-discipline went against the gospel of grace. He began to preach and write openly against Pelagius and his followers. We have a number of documents from this lengthy and heated debate. Unfortunately, most of Pelagius's arguments are preserved only in Augustine's writings against him. Many scholars believe that Augustine quoted Pelagius accurately, but we must still be aware that we are seeing this debate through the lens of only one side.

Here is an excerpt from one of Pelagius's writings as it was preserved by Augustine. Pelagius argues that God gives humans the ability to do good, but humans must choose to follow through:

> We focus on three things in order of importance. First, we put *ability*; second, *desire*; and third, *reality*. The ability has to do with our nature. The desire relates to our will. And the reality concerns what actually happens. The ability is credited to God, who gives it to his creations. The other two, desire and reality, are credited to humans. (*Grat. Chr.* 5)

Pelagius argues that for any good work to happen, a person needs the *ability* to do it and the *desire* to do it. Only then can it become a *reality*. God gives humans the *ability* to do good, but humans choose whether they *desire* to make it into a *reality*. Humans cannot do good without God's help, and God has given that necessary help to everyone.

Pelagius goes on to say, "I am free not to have a good desire or perform a good action, but I cannot claim that I am not able to have a good desire. That ability is given to me [by God]" (*Grat. Chr.* 5). No one can claim they are unable to do good, because God has given that ability, which he calls grace, to everyone. Some simply choose not to put that grace into action. At the same time, God does not force humans to choose good or evil. That is a choice of the human will.

Are humans the ultimate source of their goodness? Can humans practice asceticism by virtue of their own power and determination? No, Pelagius says, self-discipline and godly living would be impossible if God did not provide the foundational grace, the *ability*. However, God does not enact virtue for us. Human *desire* and discipline are required to make good deeds a *reality*.

Augustine rejects Pelagius's teachings because he fundamentally disagrees with some of the underlying assumptions about the nature of humanity and the human condition. Here the discussion will tie in with chapter 15 and Augustine's views on original sin. In one of his attacks on Pelagius, Augustine says,

These men are such enemies of the grace of God . . . that they believe humans can perform all the commands of God without it. . . . God simply assists us by his law and teaching so that we may learn what we ought to do and hope for, not so that we may actually do what we have learned we ought to do. (*Haer.* 88)

Augustine believes that Pelagius's views deny proper credit to God. God does not just give us a push toward doing good and then let us go on our own. Augustine argues that God also gives us the will (desire) necessary to live a holy life.

Augustine goes even farther in his attack by accusing Pelagius of making prayer pointless. If a person starts to believe or continues believing by their own will, then God has no part in it. What would be the point of prayer?

They make the prayers of the church useless, whether these are prayers that the unbelieving and those who refuse the teachings of God may return to God; or prayers for the faithful, that their faith may be increased and they may persevere. Believing or continuing to live in faith, they argue, comes from the people themselves, not from God. (*Haer.* 88)

Augustine criticizes Pelagius and his supporters for what he perceives to be the implications of their theology. Pelagius never denies the power of prayer

Courtesy of Robin M. Jensen

Figure 16.1 Cathedra of Augustine's church (Hippo). From here he delivered sermons against Pelagius and others.

or the importance of God's grace. The difference is what God's grace does in the life of the believer or unbeliever. On that issue Pelagius and Augustine disagree, as we will explore below.

Later in this passage, Augustine argues that Pelagius voids the need for infant baptism because he denies original sin: "They say infants are baptized so that by their new birth they are adopted and admitted into the kingdom of God and go from good to better. But we say we are baptized to be delivered from that ancient evil, original sin" (*Haer.* 88). Pelagius practiced infant baptism, but Augustine alleges that it was for the wrong reasons. Pelagius thinks that baptism makes infants who were already good even better, while Augustine thinks that baptism takes the infant out from under the curse of original sin.

Both sides could appeal to Scripture. Pelagius could point to 2 Peter 1:3: "His divine power has given us everything we need for a godly life through our knowledge of him who called us by his own glory and goodness." God has given us all the tools, including knowledge. But Augustine could fire back with John 15:5: "Apart from me you can do nothing." Jesus says that we can do "nothing" without God. We cannot start with a divine push and then take it from there.

Questions and Answers

Like other theological debates, this one got complicated quickly, and over time the rivals took more and more extreme positions. In order to try to clarify the assumptions and arguments on both sides, we will consider three basic questions about humanity and salvation that are critical to the debate between Augustine and Pelagius. By looking at the views of the two authors on these questions, we will more easily see why they came to dislike each other so much. You will recognize some of these ideas from our prior discussions, but perhaps it will help to approach the topic from a different angle.

◦ *What Is the Natural State of Humans?*

When human beings are conceived and come into the world, what are they like? Pelagius taught that human beings are born with the ability to have the will to do good. They may choose not to do good—they may exercise their own wills in not doing good. But that is their fault because God's grace gives them the ability to do good. Ascetics are models of people choosing to live holy lives, choosing to do what God enables them to do. God gives the *ability*, and humans need to show the *desire* (or will) to bring about the *reality*.

But for Augustine, the human will itself is completely broken for all humans for all time because of Adam's sin. Humans are conceived as sinners and are born as sinners, and God has to fix humanity through grace. Without grace, human beings have no possibility of doing good or of being right with God because the human will is broken.

Does this mean that God offers grace and then human beings respond to God's grace? No, says Augustine, the situation is even worse than that. The human condition is so bad that a person cannot receive God's grace by their own will. Receiving God's grace is also an act of God. A person does not receive God's grace because they decide to receive God's grace. They receive God's grace because God decides that they will. God causes them to receive his grace. Without God's actions, human beings have no chance. If a person demonstrates the ability and desire to bring about a reality, it is all due to God's grace. God receives all the credit.

As we can see, Pelagius and Augustine begin with conflicting ideas about the nature of humanity, and this has implications for the next question.

Why Do Some People Believe but Others Do Not?

When the gospel is preached, why do some people come to faith and others do not? A Christian family raises four children the same way, but three accept the faith and one does not. Two hundred students on a college campus crowd around a campus preacher. Some mock and jeer, while others listen and are changed. (As a college student, I saw this on The Oval at Ohio State every week when a fire-and-brimstone preacher, Brother Jed, came to campus.) How does that happen?

Pelagius argued that this was the result of human free will. Human beings have the ability to choose to accept the gospel or not to accept it. They can choose to respond to God's grace or not to respond to God's grace. Those who choose to accept God's grace and bend their desires toward his will are blessed. Others willingly refuse.

For Augustine, the answer is election. Why do some people believe and others do not? Because they are chosen (elected) by God to receive God's grace—and part of that is the grace to believe. They do not believe because they choose belief. They believe because God has chosen them, and they cannot resist.

The debates over this question were particularly heated. Augustine could argue that the notion of election is present in the Scriptures (e.g., Rom. 8:33; 9:18; 1 Pet. 2:4). Augustine's opponents could respond with other passages indicating that the offer of salvation is open to all who would receive it (e.g.,

John 3:16; Rom. 10:9–10; 2 Pet. 3:9). (Notice that parts of Romans can be used on both sides.)

What Is Grace, and How Does It Work?

Pelagius said that grace is help from God. It includes all the ways God helps humanity to be perfect, all the ways God helps us learn to do good, and all the tools God gives us to be good people. Grace includes the law of Moses. It includes the Scriptures as a whole, which teach us what God wants and help prepare us for our journey toward God and godly living. It includes the example and teaching of Christ that we see in the Gospels, a blueprint for the path we should take. Grace points us in the right direction, shows us the way to go, and gives us a running start.

Augustine said that grace is medicine for the human will (maybe we should say the antidote for the human will). The human will is broken beyond repair, so we cannot even respond to God. God's grace does what human free will cannot.

For Pelagius, grace is in a sense *external and passive*. It is offered by God from the outside but not forced on anyone. The human will is the active agent that puts God's grace into action. But for Augustine, God's grace is *internal and active*. It is not received from the outside but placed into a person by God. Grace is the active agent, the *only* agent, and the human will is passive—or more precisely, when it comes to doing good, the human will is dead.

Augustine also took the next step. If God's grace is active and the will is dead, then God must choose those who will receive grace. This led him to explore the topic of election and predestination—the idea that a person's eternal fate is *predestined* by God. While some are predestined to come to faith, others are predestined not to believe and in fact are not able to believe. In his writings Augustine focused primarily on the election of the saved, while later interpreters more explicitly discussed the plight of the condemned.

From Augustine and Pelagius to the Present

At some point for reasons that we do not know, Pelagius disappeared from the stage of history, but the debate did not stop. Augustine continued his assault on Pelagius's ideas, and a new opponent came to the forefront. Julian, the bishop of Eclanum in southern Italy (not to be confused with the pagan emperor Julian), took up the cause against Augustine after several regional church councils condemned Pelagius.

Few of Julian's writings survive, and much of what we have comes from quotations in the writings of Augustine. As you might recall from chapter 14,

Augustine was a Manichean for nine years before his eventual conversion in Milan. An element of Manichean belief was fatalism—the idea that a person's fate has been determined by forces over which they have no control. Julian picked up on this and argued that Augustine's belief in original sin and the idea of election were holdovers from the fatalism of the Manicheans. They were pagan philosophy, not Scripture. They were heresy, not Christianity. Obviously, Augustine violently disagreed and condemned Julian openly.

Even in the midst of the debates between Augustine and Pelagius and then Julian, others had already begun charting a middle course. A learned eastern monk named John Cassian had been sent to Rome as an ambassador around 404 CE, and he ended up staying in the West and founding two monasteries in southern Gaul, near Marseilles. In his *Conferences* he argued that the Pelagian and Augustinian views were both too extreme.

Cassian said that setting up a dichotomy between human free will and the grace of God was a fundamentally flawed approach from both sides of the debate. He argued that some biblical examples show God as the initial actor (Saul/Paul; Matthew the tax collector), while others suggest movement toward God on the part of the person (Zacchaeus; the penitent thief on the cross). Pelagius was wrong when he suggested that a person could be holy on the basis of their own will; free will cannot lead one to God. But Augustine went too far in denying any action of the will toward God.

Cassian suggested that, according to Scripture, God does not work the same way in every case with every person:

> By those examples that we have brought forward from the Gospel accounts, we can very clearly see that God brings salvation to humans by diverse and innumerable methods and in ways that we are not able to describe. God stirs up to greater zeal some who are already wanting and thirsting for it, while he forces others even against their will and their attempts to resist. (*Coll.* 13.17)

Both sides of the argument ignored the fact that Scripture does not provide a "one size fits all" explanation for how people come to faith. The Pelagian view gave too much credit to human free will, while Augustine's view of grace went beyond the biblical evidence. God gives grace that sometimes works with the free will that he has given humans, and sometimes overcomes it. A single explanation does not apply to every situation. That was Cassian's attempt to take a position between what he thought were extremes.

In 529 CE (about one hundred years after the deaths of Augustine and Cassian), the Second Council of Orange met in southern France to address the ongoing debates about the views of Augustine and his opponents. The council decided that Augustine was correct about original sin and the importance of grace in drawing a person to God but that he went too far in stating that some are predestined to sin and condemnation. Theologians typically describe the council's conclusions as "Semi-Augustinian."

This did not settle the debate, which came up again during the Reformation. Several of the Reformers—John Calvin chief among them—revived a more robust view of Augustine's theology of grace and election. Calvin asserted what theologians call "double predestination": "Everyone is not created in the same situation. Some are preordained for eternal life, others for eternal damnation" (*Inst.* 21.5). Both the saved and the condemned are equally predestined to their fates, so Calvin disagreed with the findings of the Second Council of Orange.

On the other side of the debate, Jacob Arminius, a Dutch theologian, questioned the biblical validity of predestination. Opponents sought to dismiss his ideas by labeling him a "Pelagian," although his theology had nothing to do with the views of Pelagius himself.

The debate continues within Protestantism to this day. Denominations in the Calvinist tradition (e.g., Presbyterians and those who bear the title "Reformed") teach divine election, while others (e.g., Methodists and Christian Churches / Churches of Christ) agree that God's grace is undeserved but believe that the offer of salvation is open to all. This latter group is often called "Arminian" by their Calvinist opponents, although their theology may have nothing to do with Arminius himself. Contemporary Lutherans and Anglicans have a strong doctrine of grace but do not go as far as the Calvinist view. No contemporary denomination known to me teaches the views of Pelagius. (At least, these are the official teachings of various denominations. Individuals may have their own views.)

The Roman Catholic Church follows Augustine's views of original sin, the Trinity, and many other topics. But they resist Augustine's view of predestination, which they think was an overreaction against Pelagius.

Orthodox Christians strongly reject Augustine's view of predestination. In fact, he is a very unpopular figure among the Orthodox because of this particular theology. When I taught in Egypt and had some Orthodox students, it was initially a challenge to get them to read Augustine with an open mind because they dislike him so much.

In the modern Christian world, few figures are as influential but also as controversial and polarizing as Augustine. This African bishop continues to cast a long shadow over Christian theology and practice.

Conclusion

The goal of this book has been to highlight significant contributions made by the early North African church that shaped the Christian world then and have continued to shape it up to today. We have seen the impact of this particular region of the continent, and we have not even discussed the importance of Egypt and Ethiopia, which have their own stories to tell.

Key Themes

Africa was at the heart of the development of early Christianity. Christians there faced the same issues as believers in other parts of the Christian world, and African thinkers and doers helped shape the responses to some of these issues. But their solutions were not always easy, and they did not always lead to harmony. Throughout this book, we have traced some of these major themes:

The response to persecution. From Perpetua to Cyprian to the Donatist Controversy, we have seen pressure put on Christian individuals and churches by periods of violent suppression. Some of the most famous martyrs of the church—Perpetua and Cyprian—came from North Africa and modeled the ultimate example of faithfulness even to the point of death. But others took a different path. Even Cyprian initially fled to protect his own life, while others chose their lives over the holy books or over what they considered a meaningless ceremony of sacrifice to the gods. In the time of Cyprian and the Donatist Controversy, the church had to deal with this variety of responses. Some argued that the church could and must remain unified, while others decided that they needed to separate themselves from those they considered impure.

The question of authority. Does authority in the church reside in an established structure of leaders, or is it more fluid than that? The story of Perpetua introduced the idea that the charismatic authority of a confessor might surpass even the authority of a bishop. That idea trickled down through history, leading to tension in the time of Cyprian and the Donatist Controversy, when bishops sought to reassert their authority over the confessors and "living martyrs." And who could be a leader? The New Prophecy (Montanist) movement that seems to have impacted Perpetua and Tertullian featured female leadership, which was not part of the official hierarchy. What should be done about that? In some cases, Christians established an alternative leadership structure because they thought that certain leaders were disqualified and perhaps threatened the legitimacy of the sacraments. The New Prophecy implicitly reflected this, but this was an explicit issue when rival bishops were elected in both Carthage and Rome in the time of Cyprian and the Donatist Controversy. Augustine, for one, was not supportive of such alternatives.

Theological developments. In terms of what we might call "technical theology," Tertullian and Augustine made major contributions. They used different metaphors, but both presented strong doctrines of the Trinity against those whom they considered schismatics and heretics, particularly Modalists. Tertullian also played a key role in the theology of the Spirit. Probably influenced by the New Prophecy, he explicitly stated that the Holy Spirit is fully God. This view was still uncomfortable for some in the Christian East nearly two centuries after the time of Tertullian, but eventually the church officially accepted the full divinity of the Spirit. Augustine had a significant impact on Western understandings of topics such as the nature and role of grace, the fallen state of humanity (original sin), and the futility of attempting to establish a spiritual kingdom on earth. Even in his own time, Augustine's ideas met with resistance, and they continue to be matters of discussion and debate today.

Relations with secular authority. The span of time covered in this book, roughly 200–430 CE, saw a dramatic reversal in the church's relationship with the Roman Empire. Perpetua and Felicity, Tertullian, Cyprian, and the Christians leading up to the Donatist Controversy lived in periods of uncertainty and sometimes violence. Apologists such as Tertullian attempted to explain Christian beliefs and practices to the outside world, hoping that their neighbors and government officials would treat Christians with more restraint. But this did not always work. Suddenly, in 311 Constantine changed the balance of power in the empire and soon after that the situation of Christians within the empire. Bishops looked to him for support and help in resolving the Donatist Controversy. For the Caecilianists, the emperor showed himself to be a champion of orthodoxy. For the Donatists, the violent actions of Constantine and some later emperors were simply the continuation of earlier violence. Imperial officials could not be trusted. Augustine lived in a more Christian context, in which the church's main problems were with heretics and "barbarians," not emperors.

Parting Thoughts for Reflection

I hope that in the process of reading this book you have gained some insights into the themes above and other more specific ideas and people that you have found interesting. As a church historian, I believe that expanding our knowledge of the past is always important.

Along the way, I have also inserted questions or statements to invite us to think about our own relationship to the past and about some of the issues that people faced, particularly ones that remain with us today. My goal has not been to convince you of *what* you should think about these issues, but I do want to convince you *that* you should think about these issues.

In that spirit, I would like to offer four final thoughts that I hope you will consider. Some are historical, others more theological These reflections apply to any book you read about history, especially church history, so the concepts are not unique to the study of the African church.

First, we are part of the universal body of Christ, the "communion of saints." The term "saints" is used here in the general sense that the apostle Paul employs, meaning all those who are "in Christ" (Rom. 1:7; 1 Cor. 1:2; 2 Cor. 1:1; Eph. 1:1; Phil. 1:1; Col. 1:2). The "communion of saints" therefore includes all believers. It includes people outside our local churches and denominations. It includes people who are worshiping the Lord across Africa, North and South America, Europe, Asia, and all other corners of the world in which people worship God and love Christ. This communion also includes those who have gone before us. It stretches across time. Those who are in Christ are full members of that community alongside Paul, Perpetua and Felicity, Tertullian, Cyprian, Caecilian, Donatus, Augustine, and Monica. We are a part of them, just as they are a part of us. They are among what the writer of Hebrews calls our "cloud of witnesses" (Heb. 12:1). And their story is our story.

As loving members of this communion, we should show them grace as we study and seek to understand their motivations and actions. Remember that we have the benefit of seeing their lives in hindsight, but they did not have that same luxury. If we show them grace, that gives us hope that future generations will also grant us grace as they look back on our lives.

Second, themes and questions may be similar, but there is no one-to-one comparison between the early African church and today. In other words, yes, we can and should reflect on the themes above, but we must remember that Decius and Diocletian are not alive today. Christians in some parts of the world are in fact dealing with threats to their lives, but many are not. The fact that a political leader favors some policies that I do not like does not mean that I am being persecuted like the early Christians were. We must also remember that the terms "Montanist," "Donatist," and "Pelagian" do not describe any modern Christian denominations. We may disagree with other Christians on their understanding of grace. Or we may believe that some denominations or parts of denominations emphasize one element of Christian theology too much or too little or that they are too strict in some way. But using the names of ancient groups as dismissive slurs for modern Christians is inaccurate and unhelpful.

Third, we must be careful not to idealize the past or to demonize the present. I grew up in a tradition in which some people thought, *We want to be like the early church, because everything was perfect then. Everyone felt the same way about everything. Everyone got along. That was so perfect. If we can get back to doing things the way they did, then we can be perfect like the early church.* By now you know that this kind of idealizing of the past is misguided. The early church was not perfect, and they did not have everything figured out. Remember that even in the time of Paul this was not the case. Most of his letters were written because churches were not united or were trying to figure out various issues. Thus, we cannot simply go to the archives of church history, pull out a pristine copy of Christianity, and "plug and play" it today. There is no perfect time that we can retrieve because early Christians were sinners too.

At the same time, we should not demonize the present. I sometimes hear Christians say things like, *I do not know how the church is ever going to survive [fill in the blank].* As we have seen in this book, at times very powerful people have proactively tried to kill the church, sometimes sporadically and sometimes in a sustained way. At other times, the church seemed to be on the brink of destruction because of internal divisions. Yet the church marched on. Yes, there are many challenges today. But as a church historian, I am convinced that our challenges are no greater than the challenges faced in the past, including those faced by the people in this book.

Fourth, as the apostle Paul writes, "He who began a good work in you will carry it on to completion until the day of Christ Jesus" (Phil. 1:6). Through many dangers, toils, and snares, the church has survived. Why? *Because the church is God's work.* No matter how much some might try to undermine or even eliminate the church, and no matter how imperfectly we operate as the church, God's work is going to move forward. It is God's work, not ours.

God has sustained the church through fire and sword from without and through threats from within. I am confident that God is going to sustain the church through the various challenges and trials that we face today.

When we understand our place within the communion of saints, we realize that we are no worse off or better off than they were in the past. We are simply living in *this time and place*, and we are "created in Christ Jesus to do good works, which God prepared in advance for us to do" (Eph. 2:10).

Select Resources
for Further Reading

Barnes, Timothy D. *Tertullian: A Historical and Literary Study*. Rev. ed. Oxford: Clarendon, 1985. Barnes proposes a timeline of Tertullian's writings and then attempts to reconstruct the development of Tertullian's thought. Audience: academic.

Bremmer, Jan N., and Marco Formisano, eds. *Perpetua's Passions: Multidisciplinary Approaches to the "Passio Perpetuae et Felicitatis."* Oxford: Oxford University Press, 2012. This is a collection of scholarly essays about various aspects of the context and interpretation of the *Passion of Perpetua and Felicity*. Audience: academic.

Brown, Peter. *Augustine of Hippo: A Biography*. New ed. Berkeley: University of California Press, 2000. Considered by many scholars to be the finest biography available on Augustine, this book is worth the effort for those with an academic bent. Be aware that Brown writes with primarily historical, not theological, interests. Audience: academic.

Burns, J. Patout, Jr. *Cyprian the Bishop*. London: Routledge, 2002. Burns explores various elements of Cyprian's writings, particularly on the issue of church unity. Audience: general.

Burns, J. Patout, Jr., and Robin M. Jensen, in collaboration with Graeme W. Clarke et al. *Christianity in Roman Africa: The Development of Its Practices and Beliefs*. Grand Rapids: Eerdmans, 2014. This volume provides a broad overview of early North African Christianity and the sources that we use to study it. It includes a rich collection of images from the region. Audience: general/academic.

Butler, Rex D. *The New Prophecy and "New Visions": Evidence of Montanism in "The Passion of Perpetua and Felicitas."* Washington, DC: Catholic University of America Press, 2006. Butler argues that elements of the *Passion of Perpetua and Felicity* clearly demonstrate elements of Montanist thought. Audience: academic.

Chadwick, Henry. *Augustine: A Very Short Introduction*. Oxford: Oxford University Press, 2001. Chadwick summarizes his expansive knowledge of Augustine in this short and accessible volume. Audience: general. Those who want a deeper dive may consider Chadwick, *Augustine of Hippo: A Life*. New York: Oxford University Press, 2009. Audience: academic.

Dossey, Lesley. *Peasant and Empire in Christian North Africa*. Berkeley: University of California Press, 2010. This book looks at Christianity in Roman Africa from the perspective of average Christians rather than bishops. The author uses a wide variety of sources, including anonymous sermons from that time that typically are overlooked. Audience: academic.

Dunn, Geoffrey G. *Cyprian and the Bishops of Rome: Questions of Papal Primacy in the Early Church*. Early Christian Studies 11. Strathfield, Australia: St Pauls, 2007. Dunn explores the relationship between Cyprian and each of the five bishops of Rome during his time as bishop of Carthage. He demonstrates Cyprian's desire to work well together but also his resistance to any Roman claim to jurisdiction outside its own province. Audience: academic.

———. *Tertullian*. London: Routledge, 2004. Dunn provides an overview of Tertullian's life and writings, accompanied by new translations of parts of Tertullian's most famous works. Audience: general.

Edwards, Mark. *Optatus: Against the Donatists*. Translated Texts for Historians 27. Liverpool: Liverpool University Press, 1997. Edwards provides a historical introduction to and translation of one of the most influential anti-Donatist works of the fourth century. Audience: general/academic.

Fitzgerald, Allan, and John Cavadini, eds. *Augustine through the Ages: An Encyclopedia*. Grand Rapids: Eerdmans, 1999. This is a large volume with articles on a wide variety of issues related to the study of Augustine. Audience: academic.

Foster, Paul, ed. *Early Christian Thinkers: The Lives and Legacies of Twelve Key Figures*. Downers Grove, IL: IVP Academic, 2010. Leading scholars present accessible introductions to important historical figures. This book features chapters on Perpetua, Tertullian, and Cyprian. Audience: general.

Frend, W. H. C. *The Donatist Church: A Movement of Protest in Roman North Africa*. Rev. ed. New York: Oxford University Press, 1985. This is a classic work on the Donatist Controversy, although many of Frend's ideas have been challenged and/or updated in more recent scholarship. Audience: academic.

Gold, Barbara K. *Perpetua: Athlete of God*. Women in Antiquity. Oxford: Oxford University Press, 2018. Gold reviews much of the previous scholarship on Perpetua, from those who treat Perpetua as a feminist hero to those who treat her as a fictional character. Audience: academic.

Harmless, William, ed. *Augustine in His Own Words*. Washington, DC: Catholic University of America Press, 2010. This book is composed primarily of passages from the writings of Augustine, translated and collected to give a beginning reader a sense of Augustine's primary concerns, particularly in his work as a bishop. Audience: general.

Heffernan, Thomas J. *The Passion of Perpetua and Felicity*. Oxford: Oxford University Press, 2012. This book provides a lengthy introduction to the text, accompanied by the Latin and Greek texts, a new translation, and commentary. Audience: academic.

Hoover, Jesse A. *The Donatist Church in an Apocalyptic Age*. Oxford Early Christian Studies. Oxford: Oxford University Press, 2018. Hoover highlights that the experience of oppression by the Donatists prompted them to focus on an expected end of the world. Audience: academic.

Lancel, Serge. *Saint Augustine*. Translated by Antonia Nevill. London: SCM, 2002. Lancel's classic work on Augustine provides more analysis of the theological elements of Augustine's life. Audience: academic.

Litfin, Bryan M. *Early Christian Martyr Stories: An Evangelical Introduction with New Translations*. Grand Rapids: Baker Academic, 2014. This book contains new translations with short introductions of a number of martyrdom texts. It includes the *Acts of the Scillitan Martyrs*, the *Passion of Perpetua and Felicity*, a passage from Tertullian, a text related to the Great Persecution, and a selection from Augustine. Audience: general.

Merdinger, J. E. *Rome and the African Church in the Time of Augustine*. New Haven: Yale University Press, 1997. Merdinger argues that the North African church—at least the Caecilianist branch—came to rely heavily on the Roman church's input on matters of internal dispute. Audience: academic.

Miles, Richard, ed. *The Donatist Schism: Controversy and Contexts*. Translated Texts for Historians 2. Liverpool: Liverpool University Press, 2016. A number of scholars explore various elements of the Donatist Controversy from its beginning through the time of Augustine. Audience: academic.

Murphy, Edwina. *The Bishop and the Apostle: Cyprian's Pastoral Exegesis of Paul*. Studies of the Bible and Its Reception 13. Berlin: de Gruyter, 2018. Murphy examines the variety of ways in which Cyprian interpreted Paul's writings for use in a pastoral setting. Audience: academic.

Oden, Thomas C. *How Africa Shaped the Christian Mind: Rediscovering the African Seedbed of Western Christianity*. Downers Grove, IL: IVP, 2007. Oden argues that past African contributions to church history can be related to the experience of the African church today. Audience: general.

Papandrea, James L. *Reading the Early Church Fathers*. New York: Paulist Press, 2012. This is a broad, accessible introduction to a wide variety of early Christian texts and authors. Audience: general.

Salisbury, Joyce E. *Perpetua's Passion: The Death and Memory of a Young Roman Woman*. New York: Routledge, 1997. Salisbury explores the tensions between Perpetua's religious identity and her cultural and family expectations. Audience: academic.

Shaw, Brent D. *Sacred Violence: African Christians and Sectarian Hatred in the Age of Augustine*. Cambridge: Cambridge University Press, 2011. Shaw examines the interaction between religious conflict and imperial ideology in the early fifth century. Audience: academic.

Still, Todd D., and David E. Wilhite, eds. *Tertullian and Paul*. Pauline and Patristic Scholars in Debate 1. New York: Bloomsbury T&T Clark, 2013. Some of the leading scholars in the world on Paul and Tertullian address various aspects of Tertullian's interpretation of Paul. Audience: academic.

Tabbernee, William. *Prophets and Gravestones: An Imaginative History of Montanists and Other Early Christians*. Peabody, MA: Hendrickson, 2009. A leading expert on Montanism presents a reconstruction of Montanist experience and practice. The stories are his constructions, but they are based on literary and archaeological evidence about real people. Audience: general/academic.

Tilley, Maureen A. *The Bible in Christian North Africa: The Donatist World*. Minneapolis: Fortress, 1997. Tilley closely studies various aspects of biblical interpretation among Donatist authors. This is an important work in collecting many of these often-ignored voices. Audience: academic.

———. *Donatist Martyr Stories: The Church in Conflict in Roman North Africa*. Translated Texts for Historians 24. Liverpool: Liverpool University Press, 1996. Tilley includes an introduction to the Donatist Controversy and translations of a variety of martyrdom accounts, including the *Acts of the Abitinian Martyrs*. Audience: general/academic.

Toom, Tarmo, ed. *The Cambridge Companion to Augustine's "Confessions."* Cambridge: Cambridge University Press, 2020. An international group of leading scholars on Augustine analyze various elements of Augustine's autobiography. Audience: academic.

Trevett, Christine. *Montanism: Gender, Authority and the New Prophecy*. Cambridge: Cambridge University Press, 2002. Trevett provides an overview of Montanism with particular attention to the role of women. Audience: academic.

Wilhite, David E. *Ancient African Christianity: An Introduction to a Unique Context and Tradition*. New York: Routledge, 2017. This is an excellent choice for those looking for a more in-depth, academic treatment of many of the topics in the book. He also covers some later material. Audience: academic.

———. *Tertullian the African: An Anthropological Reading of Tertullian's Context and Identities*. Millennium Studies 14. New York: de Gruyter, 2007. Wilhite applies various theoretical lenses to the historical context of early Christian Africa and asks what was particularly "African" about Tertullian's theology. Audience: academic.

Index

174

Index